# LEAVING CHURCH BECOMING EKKLESIA

*Because Jesus never said He would build a church*

PUBLISHED BY
KINGDOM WORD PUBLICATIONS
ALBION, MICHIGAN 49224
Printed in the U.S,A

Leaving Church Becoming Ekklesia
*Because Jesus never said He would build a church*

KINGDOM WORD PUBLICATIONS is the publishing division of THE EKKLESIA CENTER, formerly *The Center for New Testament Church Development*. The mission of Kingdom Word Publications is to produce and distribute quality books and training materials to strengthen believers who are gathering from house to house, according to the values and structure of first century Christianity.

For more information, visit our website www.TheEkklesiaCenter.org

# Acknowledgments

Any author who believes they can publish a book alone, does not understand what it takes, or is ungrateful to those who helped them along the way. The material you read is neatly arranged, but without a doubt it represents the blending of ideas, philosophies, research, sermons and teachings of so many others (Ecclesiastes 1:9). This is not plagiarism, rather, it is the revelation the author has developed based on the material he or she has received.

So it is with this book. It reflects the culmination of what the Lord has shown me, and what other writers and teachers have deposited in my spirit, from their various disciplines. More importantly, this book is more than theory. For the past two years, we have sought to live out our understanding of New Testament Christianity. It is, and continues to be a challenging, but rewarding journey. Daily we seek the Holy Spirits guidance to help us navigate the transition from a traditional church, into a network of house gatherings. We constantly pray that a door of utterance be granted to us, so that we can clearly articulate what we see the Lord doing in this day (Colossians 4:3).

Who is 'we'? Whereas, this book is the revelation the Lord gave me, it has been brought to life by those who have followed my teachings in New Life Ministries International. It takes a special people to follow a pioneering apostolic leader. I lead them into territories with no map to follow or guide us. Our journey rarely has a clear path. We see the destination, but must create the roadway to reach it. What we do as a ministry has no template. Like Paul, we move forward not depending on someone else's model of ministry made ready for us (2Corinthians 10:16).

I am so grateful for the saints in New Life Ministries International. Every month they follow my teachings, and then faithfully gather in their various homes to bring what I have taught them to life. Scripture teaches that 'without a vision, the people perish'. But I have learned that without dedicated people, the vision will perish.

Thank you New Life Ministries International. Thank you to those of you who serve on the front lines, hosting people in your homes. You edify, encourage and strengthen each other just like we read in the New Testament (Romans 16:3-5; Colossians 4:15; Philemon 1:2). Thank you, leadership team. You help me to think through the tedious aspects of this work. Without the host and the leadership team, New Life Ministries International, this book, would have no substance.

It's amazing how God connects us to people who are critical to our destiny. I have mentioned the following brothers in previous books, but I find it necessary to thank them again. Tom Wynn, Fred Anderson, Don Coleman, Dan Beaty, and Donald Todd have never ceased to encourage and advise me in this quest. They have remained steadfast in their support and prayers.

The technical aspects of this book required a team who not only know our mission, but desire to see it expressed with excellence. Thank you, Kat Wheeler, Canduace Hatman, and Margaret Generi for reading through the manuscript line by line, and word by word. You made sure that what I said in print, was exactly what I meant to say. Thanks to Joseph Kurtz, my nephew for his 'final read through' of the pre-production copy. You spotted the little things that were critical to get it right, and you gave new meaning to the phrase, 'read the small print'.

For nearly forty-four years, my wife Carolyn has been a constant source of strength and encouragement. Before any of the books I've written ever get committed to paper, she listens patiently to my thoughts and concepts — regardless of how rambling they must be at times. By the time you read this, she has heard this book dozens of times. She has seen my reactions to real life events, she has seen me walk through times of discouragement and disappointment, and watched me attempt to lead others with confidence when I was unsure of my own steps. She has allowed me to disappear many hours into my office to write and tackle projects for the ministry work. Without question, she is my greatest ally, and the source of favor that I receive from the Lord (Proverbs 18:22).

Paul wrote of his inadequacy to be called an apostle (I Corinthians 15:9). I too, find myself questioning why God chose me to be among those He is showing His intent regarding the ekklesia. Nevertheless, I am so grateful that he has given me a glimpse of His glorious plan for His people. I am convinced that in a few years, 'church' as we know it will be drastically different from what we see and experience today. I thank God for allowing me to have this little part in His plans.

Finally, I thank you, the person reading this book. I am honored that you possess it, and that you are taking the time to read its content. My prayer for you is that the Holy Spirit will 'give you the spirit of wisdom and revelation in the knowledge of Jesus Christ (Ephesians 1:17).

Blessings!
Tim Kurtz
May 2017

DEDICATED TO THOSE WHOSE QUEST FOR THE
HEART OF GOD, SUPERSEDES THE LURE OF REMAIN-
ING COMFORTABLE IN THE STATUS QUO

# TABLE OF CONTENTS

[I PRAY THAT] THE EYES OF YOUR HEART MAY BE ENLIGHTENED, SO THAT YOU MAY KNOW WHAT IS THE HOPE OF HIS CALLING, WHAT ARE THE RICHES OF THE GLORY OF HIS INHERITANCE IN THE SAINTS,

(EPHESIANS 1:18 NEW AMERICAN STANDARD BIBLE)

# INTRODUCTION

Upon this rock, I will build my…

Church – the central identifying word that encompasses the entire religious spectrum. It is the buildings we go to, the sectarian ideology we adhere to, it is the core of our spiritual identity. Church – the Body of Christ, the Bride of Christ, the called-out ones. Church – Evangelical, Pentecostal, Catholic, and Non-Denominational. Church – the guardian of doctrine, the ark for lost souls, the social bastion for the righteous. We have embraced and perpetuated a culture around this single word. A word never spoken by Jesus Christ. *Church*—a word that should have never *existed* for believers.

Jesus never said He would build a 'church'. Wait! Wait! Wait! Don't throw this book away. Don't write me off as some fringe heretic. I know what is in your bible, but give me a few pages to explain my assertion.

I started writing the framework of this book late last year. It was to be a follow up of my last book, *NO LONGER CHURCH AS USUAL*. However, I could not get the pieces to fit. Something was missing. For several months, I wrote bits and pieces of a book I originally thought to entitle, *TRANSITION: How to get the Church Where It Should Be*. It was originally intended to explore the transition from the *institutional church* into *regional house church networks*. I was internally conflicted. As I studied and meditated on what I would write, it became increasingly difficult to bring all of what was in my spirit together. It always felt like something was missing. I did not see the *house church*, per se, as being the primary goal. Leaving the big auditorium for a living room would be no more than changing from one form to another with no real focus.

> We have embraced and perpetuated a culture around this single word. A word never spoken by Jesus Christ. *Church*

I continued to read, pray, study and meditate. I also discussed this with some of my friends. Frederick L Anderson, suggested a book that he thought would interest me. I purchased and read the book and in the process, I was drawn to one of those Amazon *'people who bought this book also bought'* books. The additional book I purchased was Dean Briggs, *EKKLESIA RISING: The Authority of Christ in Communities of Contending Prayer*. It helped me to clarify the missing piece I needed. It was not just information; it became an impartation that made the transition I was attempting to articulate make sense.

Mr. Briggs' book clearly brought to light a key link that most of us have missed. With it came the clear connecting of the dots with all the pieces I have mentioned. Jesus' words at Caesarea Philippi became clear, and so did the negative implications that have resulted from misinterpreting His words. My prayer is that within the pages of this book you now hold, that you will see the big picture. My prayer is that you will grasp what Jesus intended, and make the adjustment to live out His divine purpose in your personal life, and collectively with and among other believers.

In the last paragraph of the Introduction of his book, Dean wrote,

> It is time for God's people to get a vision of the cost and glory of becoming Hell's Gates busters. Air superiority in prayer is a mission for heroes. We must identify clear targets: those supply lines and factories belching immorality, perversion and demonization into our culture. Gates of death must be brought down. Frankly, there is no other way to win. This book is about winning, which I define as **loving Christ enough to govern the Earth** in the manner intended when He commissioned His disciples in Matthew 16:18-19. (Page 11) [my emphasis added]

No one will argue that the church as we know it hasn't done many wonderful things. No one will deny that untold millions of people have been saved and have lived productive Christian lives because of the church. In 1974, the Lord saved me and I have served in the 'church' for over forty years. It is the Lord who has led me to this exciting place in life.

> No one will argue that the church as we know it hasn't done many wonderful things

My primary focus in writing LEAVING CHURCH BECOMING EKKLESIA is still about transitioning. It is about leaving wrong places, wrong thinking, and wrong processes to align with accurate kingdom ideology and purposes. It is about walking away from dead religious practices toward restoring first century values and structure. It is about transitioning from identifying with a *church system* and its well-rehearsed routines, to, as Dean said, "loving Christ enough to govern the Earth".

This book is not just about transitioning from one form to another, but transitioning from *understanding why, what, where and who* we have been, *to why, what, where and who* we should be. Whether we meet in a living room or an ornate sanctuary, we fall short of accomplishing the full will of the Father if we have not reconciled these things within ourselves by the Word of God. It is critical that we learn who we are. Scripture has made it clear. We can be nothing other than who He says we are (Ephesians 2:10). This book will explore the transitions necessary to comprehend the *why, what, where* and, most importantly, *who* we are.

As you read, remember that the expansion of the Kingdom of God in the earth is our goal. This will only be accomplished when the Body of Christ becomes mature enough to confront the forces of darkness. I believe there is a glorious future for us. We will get stronger, not weaker. We will overcome, not wait to escape. We will demonstrate the King's rule, and not acquiesce to cruel world systems.

Fasten your seatbelt, we are about to take off.

...upon this rock I will build my [ekklesia], and the gates of Hades shall not prevail against it.

(Matthew 16:18)

*Jesus never said He would build a church....*

"Transitions themselves are not the issue, but how well you respond to their challenges!"

## Jim George

Author and national speaker dedicated to helping people live a life after God's own heart

# CHAPTER I: UNDERSTANDING TRANSITION

Most of the New Testament, specifically beginning with the book of Acts is a record of transition. The law had been fulfilled in Christ, and an era of grace was beginning to manifest (Romans 8:2).

The Levitical priesthood had run its course, and through Jesus Christ the priesthood of all believers was evolving (1Peter 2:9-10). At Calvary, Jesus Christ became the final sacrifice, as a lamb slain from the foundation of the world (Revelation 13:8). The blood of bulls and goats was no longer needed (Hebrews 10:4). The temple, that had been the central place of religious activity, had become a weak shadow of its former glory. Rather than a brick and mortar

1

monolith made by human hands, the Body of Christ had become God's dwelling place (Acts 7:48-50; I Corinthians 6:19).

On the Day of Pentecost, three thousand people learned a new way to approach God. A short time later, another five thousand joined their ranks (Acts 2:41; 4:4). I would imagine that if you were to ask many of them to try and articulate what was happening, they would have been hard pressed to explain it. They just knew something exciting and powerful was taking place *in them* and *around them* because of Jesus Christ. They knew they had received a power, never experienced before under the old religious order.

The Pharisees and Sadducees, who considered themselves the religious elite in the first century, did not recognize and simply rejected the transition that was taking place. They had connived to get Jesus crucified, but within a few months they found themselves inundated with people who claimed that He had risen from the dead. They persecuted many of the followers of the new way in a futile attempt to silence them. Their tactics had little impact as the multitude of believers spread throughout the land. The Pharisees and Sadducees fought hard to maintain the religious status quo, as their world was being turned upside down. (Acts 16:20-21; 17:6; 21:28; 24:5-6).

## FRESH REVELATION AND THE STATUS QUO

Fresh revelation is the catalyst for transition. It prompts a desire to enter what should be, and the strength to leave what is. Fresh revelation never fits into the current status quo. It often challenges our religious comfort zones and forces us to re-think patterns and belief systems. Fresh revelation provides a target that keeps us focused in seasons of transition, but also a target for those who adamantly defend the traditions of men.

Fresh revelation often produces conflict. Those who have a vested interest in the current traditions and religious systems are many times the most vocal against new revelation. It was the religious leaders who resisted Jesus and the apostles (John 11:47-48; Acts 14:1-4). Jesus himself pointed out that there is only one force, one stronghold that "sets aside" and "nullifies" the revealed will of God – human traditions.[1]

Dr. Bill Hamon, in his powerful book, *The Eternal Church* wrote:

> It is one of the ironies of Church history that the persecuted participants of the former restorational movement became the primary persecutors of the next restored truth. The Jews persecuted Jesus, Judaism persecuted the Christians, the Catholics were the main persecutors of the Protestants, the historic Protestants churches persecuted the Holiness Movement, the Holiness Movement persecuted the Pentecostals, and the Pentecostals initially resisted and rejected the next restorational truth movement.
>
> Rejection of a new move comes when the previous truth participants form denominations with set creeds and doctrines. The "wineskin" of denominationalism becomes set in its ways and has no flexibility to new truth. The wineskin bursts open and many people pour out and start a new church group, which will normally end up being another

---

[1] Mark 7:1-23; cf., Frank Viola, Reimagining Church, p. 42

church organization.[2]

People who have a vested interest in old patterns often shun or reject those pursuing new horizons. Simply read the historical account of many of our cultural heroes, and you will find that many who we applaud today were ostracized and rejected when they were pursuing their vision. Close allies abandoned them. Family rejected them. Their revelation of something better caused them to swim upstream in a river filled with those who followed the current.

To some, fresh revelation is no more than 'religious information'. These people often have a '*take it or leave it*' attitude. They '*take it*' if they receive some personal benefit, but '*leave it*' if they must abandon their comfort zones. They forget that God does not give suggestions. He expects us to obey His Word. Our comfort is not His motivation — the accomplishment of His will is.

> What we consider '*fresh revelation*' is, in fact, the unveiling of God's *already* established will for this generation.

In the last days, God promised that He would pour out of His Spirit upon ALL flesh. The evidence will be dreams, visions and prophecy. Fresh apostolic and prophetic voices are beginning to release fresh insight into the purposes of God for this season (Ephesians 3:5). The pouring out of His Spirit is in effect 'God-Speaking' His purpose for His ekklesia. His purpose has already been

---

[2] W.S "Dr. Bill" Hamon *THE ETERNAL CHURCH: A Prophetic Look at the Church— Her History, Restoration, and Destiny* © 1981 Published by Destiny Image Publishers, Page 206

revealed in scripture (Genesis 1:28; Ephesians 3:10-11). However, how it will be manifested is released to us as we can handle it. What we consider *'fresh revelation'* is, in fact, the unveiling of God's *already* established will for this generation. The problem is that we often become so enamored with the last revelation that we become blinded to any new truth.

Again, fresh revelation that is new to us, has always been in the mind of God. He desires "...to make all men see what is the fellowship of the mystery, which from the beginning of the world hath been hid in God, who created all things by Jesus Christ" (Ephesians 3:9). Our carnal nature, our traditions, our fear of losing our position in the institutional church, and the god of this age, often blind us from seeing what God is doing. They keep us from hearing what He is saying. God will never stop revealing His purposes and His will. You must decide if you will hear and obey.

## THINK TRANSITION

The constant theme of this book will be that the *church* as we know it is in transition. God is orchestrating the restoration of the values and structure that birthed the *ekklesia*, not the *church*, in the first century. As you read further, prepare yourself to differentiate between what we have called church, and the ekklesia Jesus declared He would build.

What we know as 'church' must transition into what the bible calls ekklesia. This is critical. *Ekklesia* and *church* are not the same. Stop. Let me repeat this again. *Ekklesia* and *church* are not the same.

5

Ignorance of this fact has played havoc on the spiritual psyche of believers around the world. We have become something we were never intended to be.

I recently heard it said that, "Power is the ability to define a person's reality and make them accept it." Once satan distorted the identity of the ekklesia, he subtly took control of how it was intended to function. Don't misunderstand this point. Untold millions of people have been saved in the church. However, they have been, and continue to be contained in a system that is not biblical.

For nearly five hundred years, the ekklesia has been redefined and the religious masses have unknowingly, ignorantly, and sometimes willingly accepted it. Whenever we accept the enemy's definition of who we are, we are doomed to the outcome he has planned for us. This no doubt will be a tough pill for many to swallow. It bears repeating. We are not now, and were never intended to be, the 'church'. We are the ekklesia. I encourage you to do your own research. I believe that what you discover will be startling, but also invigorating.

If what I am saying is true, then we are forced to ask these questions, 'Why has ekklesia and the church been taught as being the same? Isn't ekklesia the Greek word for church? Has ekklesia or church been incorrectly translated? If so, how did the mistranslation happen? Hang on, we will explore these questions as we progress through this book.

You may be like me. I was raised 'in the church'; enjoyed and understood 'the church', and it played a significant part in my spiritual growth. Yet, I see something now that I cannot erase from my spirit.

6

It didn't come overnight. It was progressive. The Lord used the '*house church movement*' to gently move me to this point. My journey has not ended. I am no longer comfortable in the *church world* with its programs, events and controlling systems. Simultaneously, I feel somewhat as an outsider in '*house church*' circles. To paraphrase a quote from Harriet Tubman, "I [have] crossed the line. I [am] free; but there [is] no one to welcome me to the land of freedom. I [am] a stranger in a strange land".

We are entering uncharted territory. Like Abraham, we are pursuing a city whose builder and maker is God (Hebrews 11:8-10). There is no turning back. We will, and must transition from church to ekklesia. Are you ready?

We are not makers of history. We are
made by history.

Martin Luther King, Jr.

## CHAPTER 2: A GLIMPSE OF THE FIRST CENTURY

The Protestant Reformation in the 16th century set in motion the restoration of biblical truths that had been lost over the previous thirteen
hundred years. God has used remarkable men and women over the
last five hundred years to restore many of the basic doctrines that we
practice today. We tend to forget that salvation by grace through
faith, water baptism, sanctification, and the baptism in the Holy
Ghost had all but disappeared prior to the Reformation.

As foundational doctrines were restored, many of the ministry
gifts were too. However, the gifts of apostles, prophets, evangelist,
pastors and teachers were restored into a religious system that did not

exist in the first century. The elders and deacons have been adapted to fit into a religious system that was totally foreign to the early believers.

In the first century, the ekklesia was organic, but remarkably organized. It was simple, yet by no means was it frivolous. Leadership served the body as God-ordained functions, rather than hierarchal offices. Local elders and deacons provided a sense of security and continuity. Believers gathered from house to house to encourage, edify and exhort one another. The ekklesia expanded through the cities and regions, and the Word of God increased. Most importantly, Jesus Christ was the sole head of His ekklesia and the Holy Spirit effectively orchestrated the movement of human and natural resources.

In the previous chapter, I shared that the book of Acts is a record of the transition from Old Testament law into grace; and from ritual into righteousness. The Protestant Reformation of the 16th century has brought us to this season, but the journey is not complete. Let's take a trip back into the first days of the ekklesia to better understand the transition on the horizon today.

## A DAY IN YOUR LIFE – IN THE FIRST CENTURY

Imagine yourself in the first century among thousands of people from every nation who had made Jerusalem their home[1]. One morning, your daily routine is interrupted. A group of about 120 people were pouring out into the streets from the upper chambers of one of the local

---

[1] Acts 2:5

homes. What makes this interesting, is that they are all declaring the wonderful works of God to everyone who will listen; which brings up another matter.

You are standing next to a group of people from another nation, and it seems that both of you can clearly understand what the group from the upper room was saying — even though you all speak different languages. How could that be?[1]

It is such a spectacle that some in the crowd begin mocking them, saying they are drunk. Then, one from the group, assumingly the leader, finds a place to stand up before the crowd and begins explaining what you are witnessing.

"Men of Judea, and all who dwell in Jerusalem," he shouted. "Listen to what I am saying. These men are not drunk as you suppose, as it is only the third hour of the day." There was some laughter in the crowd. He went on to say, "But this is what was spoken by the prophet Joel." You watch as the crowd begins to settle down to hear his seemingly impromptu speech. The atmosphere turns more serious as he continues. "And it shall come to pass, says God, that in the last days I will pour out of My Spirit on all flesh..." By now the crowd is absorbed in what this man is saying.[2]

For several minutes, he shares much of what you know historically, but had never imagined it coming to life. How compelling it is for you to hear him remind you of Jesus, who you knew had been

---

[1] Acts 2:8-12

[2] Acts 2:14-17

publicly crucified less than two months prior to this. You probably had never considered the irrefutable connection between Jesus and David. Like many, you were waiting for the Messiah, and it appeared from the prophetic words of David he quoted, that He had come, but it was possible you may have missed Him.[1]

His words were penetrating. I would like to have seen the look on your face, when the man who was speaking declared that Jesus, the one who had been crucified, was alive, and that he and all those who were with him had seen Him. You would probably be shaken to your core. As you stand there trying to process what was said, you hear many around you begin to cry out, "What must we do?"[2]

"Repent, and let everyone of you be baptized in the Name of Jesus, for the remission of sins, and you shall receive the Gift of the Holy Ghost", he answered. "For the promise, (that you were witnessing being demonstrated in them), was to you, your children and any future generation who call on the Name of the Lord."[3] What happened next would no doubt be indelibly etched into your spirit for the rest of your life. Without hesitation, the rest of the day was spent as you, and thousands more repented, called on the Name of the Lord, and were baptized in Jesus' Name.[4]

---

[1] Acts 2:27-32

[2] Acts 2:37

[3] Acts 2:38-41

[4] See Acts 2:19-46

The days that followed were filled with excitement for you. Something had happened in you, and in nearly everyone you knew. You would gather with others like yourself, usually in each other's homes, praising God, encouraging and sharing this phenomenal event with one another. Discussion may have wafted from the excitement of the event, to how to get the word out to others, hopefully, without raising the ire of the Roman government.

You probably had no way of knowing that three thousand people had been impacted on that day. All you knew is that your life, and the lives of so many others had been changed. Of course, you would have no way of knowing that nearly thirty years later, a Jewish proselyte physician would explain this event to his friend, that the Lord was *adding to His congregation* daily those who were being saved.[1] All you knew is that the excitement continued to grow as more and more people began to call on the Name of the Lord Jesus Christ, who had risen from the dead.

> ...the excitement continued to grow as more and more people began to call on the Name of the Lord Jesus Christ, who had risen from the dead

No doubt, you noticed that the religious leaders tried to stop what was happening. It was obvious that they were at a loss as to how to stop this phenomenal change in so many people. You probably wondered why they rejected such notable miracles like the beggar who

---

[1] Acts 2:47 Ekklesia was translated as *congregation* in the Tyndale Bible published in the 16th century

was healed after being lame all his life. Nevertheless, you embraced this wonderful change and so did many others.[1]

## SOMETHING YOU DIDN'T SEE

The leaders of this new movement were unorthodox. They did not demand that you adhere to the religious customs that you had previously been taught were necessary. These men, who had personally lived with Jesus Christ, performed miracle after miracle and made it clear that everything they did was in the Name of the risen Lord.

With so many followers of this new way, it would seem logical that they would have tried raising enough money to erect temples to gather the people into one place. No. Instead, they encouraged you all to love one another, edify one another, serve one another, and pray for one another. They were more concerned that you, and all new believers, were filled with the power of the Holy Spirit like they were.[2] But why did they choose not to build temples or special meeting places? A clue to their thinking was given in the most unlikely situations and places.

The apostles (as they had become known), were now watching over thousands of new believers eager to follow the ways of the risen Christ. People were sharing resources to the point where it was reported that no one among them lacked anything.[3] That is, until some

---

[1] Acts 3:1-26; 4:1-4; 5:14; 11:24

[2] Acts 8:17; 10:44-48; 11:14-18; 19:6

[3] Acts 4:33-35

14

of the Greek women were being neglected in the daily distribution of goods. Rather than trying to micro-manage this problem, the apostles established criteria for the people to choose seven men who could handle this matter. One of the men chosen was Stephen who was known as a man of faith and full of the Holy Spirit.[1]

No one knows how long it took Stephen and the other six chosen to resolve the problem with the Grecian widows, but it was obvious that soon he began doing signs and wonders among the people. It was remarkable to see an average believer, demonstrate the same power and authority that had previously only been demonstrated by the apostles.[2]

Some of the religious leaders were clearly angered by the power Stephen demonstrated. They tried to trip him up with various arguments, but were unable to refute his Holy Spirit led wisdom. So, they resorted to lying and conjuring up stories to get him arrested. It is his defense before the religious council that brings us back to the issue of why the apostles never pursued erecting dedicated buildings for worship.[3]

Beginning with Abraham, Stephen began to lay an historical foundation for the risen Christ. Through Jacob, Moses, and even Solomon he skillfully rehearsed facts that no respectable religious leader

---

[1] Acts 6:1-5

[2] Acts 6:8

[3] Acts 6:9-15

would try to refute. It was when he spoke of David that the mood took a turn for the worse. Stephen shared how David desired to build a house for the Lord and how God chose Solomon to complete the task. But during this Stephen made a unique statement. He said, "...the Most High does not dwell in temples made with hands..." He then quoted the prophet Isaiah. "Heaven is my throne, and the earth is my footstool. What house will you build for me? ...or what is the place of my rest?" (Isaiah 66:1)

This last question not only helped to fuel the anger of the religious council, but it gives us a peek into why the apostles did not pursue physical buildings. They understood that we – collectively and individually – the Body of Christ – were the dwelling place of the Most High. God was no longer contained in man-made tabernacles, behind veils, accessible only by the High Priest (Hebrews 9:7-8).

When Christ died on the cross, the veil in the temple was torn from top to bottom; and access to the Holy of Holies, to the presence of God, was available to all. Throughout the entire New Testament, there was never an attempt by believers to restrict God to a dedicated building. Believers could gather in groups as small as two or three, or in private homes and demonstrate more power than all the religious elite combined.[1]

The religious council stoned Stephen to death. Ironically, there

---

[1] Acts 4:31 the gathering place was shaken by their prayers. Acts 12:5 the ekklesia prayed and set forth the miraculous release of Peter from jail. Acts 16:16 the worship and prayers of Paul and Silas shook the jail and freed everyone.

was a young man by the name of Saul who witnessed this brutal execution. It was this same young man who would later bring clarity to the New Testament temple with a simple question. "Don't you know that your body is the temple of the Holy Spirit?"[1]

## WHAT DOES THIS MEAN TODAY?

The Day of Pentecost dramatically introduced the presence and infilling of the Holy Spirit to everyday people. If this had been an Old Testament event, you would probably have only read about one man (i.e. Moses, Elijah, Samuel, etc.) who would have been anointed by God to carry out some supernatural act. But on this day, a hundred and twenty were filled with the Holy Ghost and when they poured out into the streets, another three thousand lives were quickly impacted. Yes, God confirmed that He was pouring out of His Spirit on all flesh (Joel 2:28; Acts 2:17). This is what makes the story of Stephen so interesting.

Stephen was not an apostle. He was simply a believer who was recognized for being full of faith and the Holy Ghost; a trait that should be in each of us. We could concentrate solely on the fact that he was martyred for his faith, but I suggest that it is important to pay attention to what originally drew the ire of the Libertines, Cyrenians, Alexandrians and those from Cilicia and Asia. In Acts 6:8, it is recorded that Stephen did great wonders and miracles among the people. It was the manifestation of the Holy Ghost that ruffled the feathers

---

[1] I Corinthians 16:19

of the religious elite. Was Stephen an exception? Are there other examples of ordinary believers doing extraordinary things? Yes.

Another one of the seven men chosen to resolve the Grecian
widow problem was Philip. In Acts, chapter eight, we find him
preaching in Samaria. He too performed miracles, cast out devils and
healed the lame (Acts 8:6-8). Later, Philip preached Jesus to an Ethi-
opian eunuch. Immediately after baptizing the eunuch, Philip was mi-
raculously transported to another place. Philip was known as an evangelist who had four daughters that prophesied (Acts 21:8-9). Scripture did not say they were Prophetess. They were simply four girls
who prophesied.

Isn't it amazing that Ananias, a disciple, a devout man according
to the law, was chosen by God to lay hands on Saul so that he could
be healed of his blindness (Acts 9:9-18; 22:12)? Ananias was simply
a Jewish brother who had a good reputation among his peers. The
more you consider the Word of God, the more you will see that it is
God's intent that *all* believers be endued with power from on high.

> And now, Lord, behold their threatenings: and *grant unto thy servants,*
> *that with all boldness they may speak thy word, By stretching forth*
> *thine hand to heal; and that signs and wonders may be done by the*
> *name of thy holy child Jesus.* And when they had prayed, the place was
> shaken where they were assembled together; *and they were all filled*
> *with the Holy Ghost, and they spake the word of God with boldness.*
> (Acts 4:29-31)

Apostles Peter and John had been threatened by the high priest
for preaching the power and resurrection of Jesus Christ. When they

were released, they went back to their own company of believers and told all that had happened to them. Then they prayed. In their prayer, they asked the Lord to grant to his servants boldness to speak the word, and that healing, signs and wonders would be done in the Name of Jesus. When I first read this account, I assumed that Peter and John were requesting boldness and the manifestation of miracles be done for themselves. However, when you read the entire story, it becomes clear that such is not the case.

Remember, Peter and John were reporting to their fellow believers what had been said and done to them by the high priest. The religious elite had attempted to silence them, but these two apostles *boldly* withstood them (Acts 4:13-19). This makes it clear that Peter and John did not need to pray for their own boldness. When they prayed, they were praying primarily for the believers who had gathered with them. They asked the Lord to give them the same boldness they had to speak the Word. What was the result?

> And when they had prayed, the place was shaken where they were assembled together; <u>and they were all filled with the Holy Ghost, and they spake the word of God with boldness.</u> (Acts 4:31)

Everyone in the room was filled with the Holy Ghost, and everyone in the room began to speak the Word of God with boldness. Individually, they were filled with power. Collectively, they could form an ekklesia, with the power to change their region. I do not doubt that some of these believers began to demonstrate healing, miracles, signs, and wonders. This is exactly what Jesus declared should happen.

And *these signs shall follow them that believe*; In my name shall they cast out devils; they shall speak with new tongues; They shall take up serpents; and if they drink any deadly thing, it shall not hurt them; they shall lay hands on the sick, and they shall recover. (Mark 16:17-18)

Signs follow believers. Let that sink in for a moment. Signs follow believers. Signs are not contingent upon denominational affiliation or by what sacred title you are known. Signs follow believers. Nowhere in scripture has the evidence of signs and wonders, healing and miracles been done away with. Signs follow believers. The lack of signs and wonders, miracles and healing in this age is not because God has changed what He does; it is because there is a lack of believers in the earth. Signs follow believers. This will help you to understand the present truth being released into the earth in this season; a truth that is vital to your personal destiny, a truth that is critical to understanding ekklesia.

**The present truth being established in the earth is to fully release the saints to do the work of ministry (Ephesians 4:12).**

This is a major shift. It will have a profound impact on nearly everything we do. The ekklesia cannot operate like the church has for so many years. The *form* changes only as our *understanding* changes. In the coming years, the gathering of believers will become more defined by scripture, rather than historical practices.

This is the day of the saints. The Lord's focus is His original intent when He placed man in the Garden to keep it and tend it. The mandate to be fruitful, to multiply and replenish the earth, to subdue it and have dominion is the divine focus (Genesis 1:28). The ministry gifts Jesus gave when He ascended were commissioned to equip the saints for this work of ministry (Ephesians 4:11-12). Like Peter and John, who prayed that all those who gathered with them would be granted boldness and the ability to perform signs and wonders, so it is with the ministry gifts. They should be equipping the saints and praying that they be empowered with boldness, and sent forth to minister in the earth with signs and wonders. The power of the ekklesia is fueled by believers who are empowered by the Holy Spirit to do great exploits in the Kingdom of God (Daniel 11:32).

What you and I do over the next few years will fuel the transitions necessary to expand the Kingdom of God in the earth. Let's examine some of the necessary transitions that must, and will soon take place.

Change is the law of life. And those who look only to the past or present are certain to miss the future.

John F. Kennedy

## CHAPTER 3: NECESSARY TRANSITIONS

The 'church' as we know it will undergo a major change over the next ten years. Whereas this may sound prophetic, it is in reality, a response to looking at the social, political and economic environment of our country and the world. Unfortunately, the 'church' has not been effective in countering the onslaught of evil and corruption sweeping the globe. Instead, the 'church' in general has tried to fit into society. Many church systems have compromised biblical standards and acquiesced to the worlds culture. The result is, the church looks confused and disconnected.

Transitioning is not to be confused with the futile attempts churches implement to try and reinvent themselves. Many 'churches' have created a plethora of service styles to fill their pews. Contemporary, traditional, youth, seeker-sensitive, deliverance and prophetic services are often accompanied by light shows, crisp musicians, dramatic presentations, videos, and blaring sound systems. The result is a religious populous who are soulishly entertained but spiritually anemic.

The coming transition has one primary goal; *to empower and release the saints to do the work of ministry* (Ephesians 4:12). That is the core purpose of this transition. What Jesus said He would build cannot be done with people who are contained within religious systems. They must be given free rein to accomplish whatever assignment Jesus Christ, the Commander-In-Chief has for them. This by no means is advocating a religious free-for-all. It is not by-passing the ordained leadership He has established for the ekklesia. The elders, deacons and five-fold ministry gifts are vital to strengthen and train an effective and orderly army of believers.

As believers begin to understand that the church must become the Lord's ekklesia, there will be five critical areas that will simultaneously experience some form of transition. I believe these transitions will take place over the next ten years. As you read through them, take time to reflect on where you are now. Think about how these transitions will impact you personally and the church as you know it.

## TRANSITION AREA 1: THE TRADITIONAL METHOD OF GATHERING WILL TRANSITION

The 'church building' mindset is a containment mindset. We have been trained to believe that meeting weekly in a dedicated building has had more appeal and correctness, than gathering from house to house.

In a dedicated building, you have a few elite players controlling the masses. Most people who enter are spectators, not participants.

Within the institutional church system, conformity is an unwritten rule. Most churches are part of a denominational sect. The beliefs and rules of conduct have been passed down from generation to generation. A person is considered a 'member' in good standing if they pay their tithes, regularly attend public meetings, and who follow, usually without question, the denominational party line.

Gathering in dedicated buildings is a combination of Old Testament temple worship and pagan methodologies. Church people revere their building sanctuary as holy. They give hyper-religious lip service to the fact that their body is the temple of the Holy Spirit, but treat their 'church' building as Moses did the Tabernacle or Pharisees treated the Temple (Isaiah 29:13; ICorinthians 3:16). Among some church groups, the stage area is treated as the Holy of Holies; women and children aren't allowed to be on it. I have heard the pulpit referred to as 'the sacred desk', and the pulpit area itself is often adorned with throne like chairs for the 'clergy'.

> Gathering in dedicated buildings is a combination of Old Testament temple worship and pagan methodologies

It doesn't take much research to find that the buildings and much of what is done on Sunday mornings is drawn out of the third and fourth century pagan playbook. Innocent believers have had no reason to question or investigate the fact that everything from the steeple to the stain glass windows have some origin in paganism. Anti-Christian

25

groups are using these facts to attempt to confuse and weaken the faith of many believers. The auditorium style setting plays right into this satanic trap. It keeps the masses spiritually weak and dependent. It is designed to minimize participation from the believers and focus more on those performing on the stage. This arrangement is acceptable in the church, but unacceptable to the ekklesia.

My previous book, NO LONGER CHURCH AS USUAL, focused primarily on the 'house church'. If we aren't careful, gathering from house to house can become just as ineffective as large gatherings in dedicated buildings. I believe New Testament biblical evidence supports small house gatherings and that they should be encouraged and supported. We must be careful, however, not to morph into worshipping the house to house gatherings as a style of worship deemed to be superior than dedicated buildings.

The small house gatherings encourage believers to edify, exhort and comfort one another. The small house gatherings provide the atmosphere for believers to explore their gifts in a safe environment. The small house gathering is where believers can live out the over fifty 'one-another' verses in scripture. The small house gatherings can be the 'two or three' who gather with the guarantee of Christ being in their midst (Matthew 18:20). Most importantly, those who gather in homes can easily identify demonic gates in their homes, neighborhoods, cities, schools, and local government that need to be destroyed.

> The breaker is come up before them: they have broken up, and have passed through the gate, and are gone out by it: and their king shall pass before them, and the LORD on the head of them. (Micah 2:13)

With Jesus Christ, as the Head of a divine battering ram, these gatherings can smash through enemy strongholds. Demonic gates of poverty, immoral sex, greed, corrupt politics and more can be destroyed. Multitudes of ekklesia that gather from house to house can turn regions upside down in targeted fervent prayer.

## CULTURAL AND SOCIAL CHANGES

Socially, the Millennials and Generation Xers are expecting more authenticity from their worship experience. A report by the Pew Research Center[1], and numerous online articles point to a consistent decline in 'church' attendance. The reasons given are widespread. Whether it be social commitments, job related issues, ease of access to online or television religious programming, or sporting events, the traditional form of gathering in auditoriums is losing its appeal.

Many denominations are shrinking. This is in effect emptying out many dedicated buildings. People are leaving with nowhere to go. Some are being drawn into alternative religions. Unfortunately, many 'church leaders' point to those leaving as the problem. They have not come to grips with the fact that it is most likely the church system that is the culprit. I personally noted that in several of the articles and books that I read on this subject, the goal of the author was to suggest ways to combat the declining attendance *and salvage the system.* Allow me to show you why I believe that is the wrong approach.

------

[1] The Pew Forum on Religion & Public Life *"Nones" On The Rise: One-in-Five Adults Have No Religious Affiliation* © 2012 Pew Research Center

First, to combat declining attendance by creating ways to retain people, assumes that the system is superior to the needs of the people. It suggests that an individual's spiritual growth is contingent upon their attendance to meetings sponsored by the church system. Even small group gatherings are monitored and controlled by the larger church system leadership.

I accepted the Lord in February of 1974. A common admonishment was, if I wanted to grow in the Lord, I needed to "Sit under the teaching". I have been living for the Lord over 43 years. I still treasure good biblical teaching. Yet, I know people who have been 'sitting under the teaching' for as many years as I have been saved, and their spiritual growth is tragically stunted. The system locks them into a world where spiritual growth is measured by activity and promotion within itself — not by effectiveness in real world issues.

Second, retention usually means conformity. Too often individualism and independence is frowned upon as 'rebellion' in the institutional church system. Dr. Josh Packard made this observation regarding 'Dones'[1] in his book, *Church Refugees*[2]. He states that the Dones feel the way that "*...the institutional church tries to construct community by focusing on uniformity over unity, is counterproductive to what they feel is true and authentic community.*" At nearly every Billy Graham crusade, his altar appeal is accompanied by the famous hymn, Just As I Am. We often chuckle that many denominations take the

---

[1] Dones are generally described as those who have made an intentional decision to leave institutional and organized religious systems, but not their faith in the Lord Jesus Christ.

[2] CHURCH REFUGEES *Socialogist Reveal Why People Are Done With Church but Not Their Faith* © 2015 Josh Packard and Ashleigh Hope Published by group.com

title of this song literally. In other words, when you join them, the leadership says become '*just as I am*' to be successful among us.

Third, trying to salvage the system fosters religious competition as churches vie to fill their pews. I have driven through several big cities, and find it amazing the number of billboards promoting churches in the area. Each of them has the smiling face of the 'pastor' or the 'pastor and his wife' along with a fancy slogan implying that their church is the best place to worship. They are all trying to lure people into their sanctuaries or worship centers, and attempting to keep them with their version of the Gospel. They offer tantalizing worship shows that they secretly hope is better than the worship show in the church down the street. Their portrayal of Jesus Christ is the main feature. Their hope is that those who visit (usually from another church), will join their ranks. Sadly, this is believed to be evangelism.

Small churches are equally as guilty. Transfer evangelism is rampant among them, too. Some use their size as a sign of spiritual martyrdom. They declare that they preach such hard-hitting truth that people shy away from them in lieu of the glitzy weak messages of the larger churches. Simultaneously these same church leaders will attend 'church growth' seminars and conferences looking for a way to become like the mega churches they have criticized. Thus, they fall into the trap of competing with the small church down the street. Religious competition will continue as long as we believe that Jesus came to build a church.

The fruit of religious competition is a false version of evangelism. Earlier I alluded to the fact that many churches grow by 'transfer' evangelism. That is when a person leaves one church to join another. I have seen a tremendous lapse in integrity among church leaders in this area. This has led to a form of pseudo-discipling where accommodation replaces transformation. I have watched people steeped in drugs, illicit sexual behavior, and moral deviancy leave one church and become a leader in another. There is no evidence of them having a transformative relationship with Jesus Christ, but rather a skill that their new church wanted. This practice alone sends a horrible message to the world.

To survive, church systems need people. More people equate to more financial resources. The system needs a constant influx of money to survive. The more people you have, the more potential money you have to pay salaries, maintain buildings, and underwrite programs and events. That would be very crass to admit openly, but it is a fact lurking underneath the surface. This leads us to the next transition on the horizon.

## TRANSITION AREA 2: WE MUST TRANSITION IN OUR USE OF FINANCIAL AND HUMAN RESOURCES

The flow of money has become the driving force behind most churches. Outwardly, all churches claim that winning souls is their top priority. But that purpose is muddied when their survival as an organization is threatened. Many times, you must question their real motivation behind programs and events. You simply need to follow the money trail.

Before I go further, I must interject that I thoroughly understand that money is needed to accomplish many things. I am not so naive to believe that ministry does not need financial support. My point is that resources will have greater impact if they are distributed today as they were by the first century ekklesia – in practice and principle.

A common argument is that, "We are living in different times." Yes, I agree that we are, but this means we should be more vigilant in understanding how to become good stewards of all that God provides. Consider the fact that the bible records no money among the first century ekklesia was ever collected to support a building fund. Compare the billions of dollars spent on dedicated church buildings, with the fact that believers in the first century simply gathered in homes and public places. Very little money was collected to support local or itinerant ministers. Compare the lifestyle of the first century apostles and itinerant ministers with the salaries and perks received by church leaders today. There is no comparison in either principle or practice. Consider that most money was used to assist poorer saints. The modern 'church' will easily send someone to the government for help, without considering the fact that believers in the first century gave in such a way that it was said that no one lacked among them. This should make you think. It is not the issue of money; it is how we have chosen to use it that should concern us.

> ...no money among the first century ekklesia was ever collected to support a building fund

## PERSONAL DISCLOSURE

In my ministry journey, I have personally been the recipient of a salary and some perks from the church. From time to time, the fellowship I now serve occasionally gives me a small stipend. When I received the salary, it was part of the budget and considered payment for the work I did for the church. Today, when I receive a contribution, it is to support my ministry work. It comes when it comes. There is no pressure on the fellowship to provide me anything. I work full time to meet the needs of my wife and I, and will continue to do so until the Lord says otherwise. I share this because I understand financial compensation to church leadership can be the greatest hindrance to transitioning from church to ekklesia. Frederick L. Anderson put it succinctly, "It is hard to get a man to understand something, whose livelihood depends on him not understanding it."

The transition from a church mindset to an ekklesia mindset will impact how resources are used. Our stewardship goal is to please our King, the Lord Jesus Christ. There is no way to outline how every resource will be used. However, there are biblical patterns and examples that will help us determine the heart of the Father.

## GIVING TO THE POOR AMONG US

> Then the disciples, every man according to his ability, determined to send relief unto the brethren which dwelt in Judaea: (Acts 11:29)

> For it hath pleased them of Macedonia and Achaia to make a certain contribution for the poor saints which are at Jerusalem. (Romans 15:26)

The care of the poor saints should be at the top of our list. The local, regional, and national needs of our brothers and sisters should be first in our giving priorities. Remember, the ekklesia is a living organic entity made up of believers, who give willingly to help insure that 'no one lacks' among them. That may be why Paul instructed believers to 'distribute to the necessity of the saints' (Romans 12:13; 1Corinthians 16:1; 2Corinthians 9:1, 12)

Jesus said that the poor will always be among us (Deuteronomy 15:11; Mark 14:7). Giving to the poor in our communities, region and the world should be another focus of our giving. We should always be ready to meet the needs of the less fortunate. However, I want to

> ...the ekklesia is a living organic entity made up of believers, who give willingly to help insure that 'no one lacks' among them

caution that our giving should not become a 'welfare' program giving indiscriminately to anyone who has his or her hand out. Some believe we should give to the poor without restrictions. I disagree. Along with stewarding, is discernment. It is not wise to pour money and resources into those who willfully squander it. Giving money to anyone who mismanages and wastes their resources only exacerbates their problem. The value of no one lacking among us is to help insure that believers have the resources they need to fulfill their ministry. All giving should clearly be a benefit to the Kingdom of God.

## GIVING TO INSTRUCTORS

Let him who receives instruction in the Word [of God] share all good things with his teacher [contributing to his support]. (Galatians 6:6 Amplified Bible[1])

---

Paul instructed believers to share financially with those teaching them. The passage above in The Phillips Translation says, 'the man under Christian instruction should be willing to contribute toward the livelihood of his teacher'. Such giving is voluntary and should never be a prerequisite for ministry service. Intra-itinerant and itinerant ministers should seek ways to be self-supporting. They must be willing and prepared to serve the Body of Christ without any financial remuneration. Their motive must be the building and edifying of the believers. Whatever donation is given to them must be received with thanksgiving and accepted as sufficient (Philippians 4:11-12).

## MONEY LAID AT THE APOSTLES' FEET

In the early days following Pentecost, believers gave generously, and scripture declares that no one lacked among them. What first appears to be a single incident of laying resources at the Apostles' feet may have been a consistent form of giving. This type of giving must be understood because a severely dysfunctional version of 'laying money at the apostles' feet' has crept into the modern church.

> And the multitude of them that believed were of one heart and of one soul: neither said any of them that ought of the things which he possessed was his own; but they had all things common. And with great power gave the apostles witness of the resurrection of the Lord Jesus: and great grace was upon them all. (Acts 4:32-33)

Laying resources at the apostles feet began with the attitude of the believers. They were of one heart and one soul. There was a common belief that individual possessions belonged to the Body of Believers. I want to emphasize that this was not an early form of communism or socialism, but rather a spiritual COMMON-ism that existed among

34

the believers. Everyone seemed to make their personal goods available for the benefit of the community of believers. I believe this includes financial and material resources as well as skills and talents.

> Neither was there any among them that lacked: for as many as were possessors of lands or houses sold them, and brought the prices of the things that were sold, And laid them down at the apostles' feet: and distribution was made unto every man according as he had need. And Joses, who by the apostles was surnamed Barnabas, (which is, being interpreted, The son of consolation,) a Levite, and of the country of Cyprus, Having land, sold it, and brought the money, and laid it at the apostles' feet. (Acts 4:34-37)

No one lacked among them. Let that thought sink into your spirit. Try to imagine regions of believers wherein no one lacks among them. Imagine a body of believers where every need is met. If it is written in the Word of God, then it is possible to experience. 'No one lacking...' was a result of the spirit embraced by the entire community of believers. They believed their possessions were part of the whole community. They had all things in common. Implicit in that belief was the desire that no one should lack among them. This core belief prompted them to act. Those who had excess properties and land sold them and laid the proceeds at the apostles' feet.

According to the Jamieson, Fausset and Brown Bible Commentary, the act of laying something at someone's feet was most likely a figurative term that implies something that was committed to another's care.[1] In other words, when people laid resources at the apostles' feet, they fully entrusted them to handle the proper disposition of

---

[1] Acts 4:35 Jamieson-Faussett-Brown Bible Commentary © 1996 Hendrickson Publishers Marketing, LLC

their giving. What the apostles did with the money was as important as this act of giving itself. This is where error has crept into the modern version of 'laying money at the apostles' feet'.

The money collected was not used for the benefit of the apostles. The money did not support the extravagant lifestyles of church leaders. The selling of houses and lands, and the subsequent distribution of the proceeds was not done at the request of the apostles. It was the free-will act of believers who obviously saw needs among their brothers and sisters. The apostles understood that they were entrusted with resources that were not intended for their personal benefit. These resources were given for needs among the people; modern day 'apostles' need to take note of this fact. Whenever people put money at an apostle's feet, it is for the needs of believers.

Second, it appears that the money that was donated was from excess goods sold by the believers. They sold houses and lands. It did not appear to come from the donor's regular source of income. This was a special offering prompted by the Holy Spirit. I believe this form of giving was ongoing and not just a onetime event. As believers were led to sell excess items, the proceeds were willingly given to the apostles for distribution. This explains why the lies of Ananias and his wife Sapphira were so grievous (Acts 5:1-11). They lied to the Holy Ghost. They tried to tempt the Spirit of the Lord by holding back a part of what they had sold. The sad irony is that they were not required to give anything. To give or not to give was their choice, and there was no need for them to lie (Acts 5:4). This sin cost them their lives.

---

Today, donations 'laid at the apostle's feet' should follow the same pattern demonstrated in the first century. This form of giving should be prompted by the Holy Spirit and come from the selling or donation of excess goods (i.e. property, houses, cars, clothing, etc.). It should always be voluntary. No one should ever be compelled or manipulated to give in this manner. The funds should be distributed among the saints as needs arise.

## GIVING TO ELDERS

> Let the elders that rule well be counted worthy of double honour, especially they who labour in the word and doctrine. For the scripture saith, Thou shalt not muzzle the ox that treadeth out the corn. And, The labourer is worthy of his reward. (1 Timothy 5:17-18)

Paul implied that financial compensation to elders that ruled well, was in order. He said they should be considered worthy of double honor. The Greek phrase used for double honor (diplous time) in I Timothy 5:17 refers to giving double value. When it is combined with verse 18, it is obvious that Paul is speaking about financial remuneration. Unfortunately, some have twisted this passage to suggest the 'senior pastor' should be paid twice the salary of the highest paid member of the church. This is an erroneous and self-serving interpretation, especially when you understand that the concept of a 'senior pastor' was nonexistent in the first century.

When you consider the whole counsel of scripture, Paul specifically encouraged elders to be self-supporting. He personally set the example.

> And from Miletus he sent to Ephesus, and called the elders of the [ekklesia]. And when they were come to him, he said unto them, Ye know, from

the first day that I came into Asia, after what manner I have been with you at all seasons, Serving the Lord with all humility of mind, and with many tears, and temptations, which befell me by the lying in wait of the Jews: And how I kept back nothing that was profitable unto you, but have shewed you, and have taught you publickly, and from house to house, (Acts 20:17-20)

I have coveted no man's silver, or gold, or apparel. <u>Yea, ye yourselves know, that these hands have ministered unto my necessities, and to them that were with me. I have shewed you all things, how that so labouring</u> ye ought to support the weak, and to remember the words of the Lord Jesus, how he said, It is more blessed to give than to receive. (Acts 20:33-35)

Peter admonished the elders to serve and shepherd the flock of God willingly, and not for 'filthy lucre'.

The elders which are among you I exhort, who am also an elder, and a witness of the sufferings of Christ, and also a partaker of the glory that shall be revealed: Feed the flock of God which is among you, taking the oversight thereof, not by constraint, <u>but willingly; not for filthy lucre</u>, but of a ready mind; (1Peter 5:1-2)

Jesus warned that some leaders are no more than hirelings. They don't have the interest of the flock in their hearts and they will abandon it when trouble arises.

But he that is an hireling, and not the shepherd, whose own the sheep are not, seeth the wolf coming, and leaveth the sheep, and fleeth: and the wolf catcheth them, and scattereth the sheep. The hireling fleeth, because he is an hireling, and careth not for the sheep. (John 10:12-13)

Elders should never serve for money. If they are given financial gifts by the local [ekklesia], they should receive it with humility. They should not allow gifts to damage their impartiality in serving. This explains why Paul warned against appointing a novice as an elder. A novice would not know how to handle financial blessings; a novice could easily become caught in the trap of covetousness (1 Timothy 3:6). Mature elders who rule well should be counted worthy of double honor by the [ekklesia] they serve.

## CONSIDERING GIFTS TO OTHERS

In his defense of his apostolic ministry, Paul challenged the Corinthian believers about giving financially to his ministry. In the process of making his case, he made the following statement:

> Do ye not know that they which minister about holy things live of the things of the temple? and they which wait at the altar are partakers with the altar? Even so hath the Lord ordained that they which preach the gospel should live of the gospel. (1Corinthians 9:13-14)

Paul was referring to the Old Testament priesthood; wherein, the Levites received the tithes and offerings from all Israel for their care (Leviticus 6:25-26; Numbers 5:9-10). Unlike the other tribes, the Levites did not receive an inheritance of land. God Himself, was their inheritance (Deuteronomy 10:9). Their work began with the Tabernacle in the wilderness and continued in the temple. The Levites consisted of more than Aaron's sons, who served as the primary priests. There were many families among the Levites, who served in various capacities (Numbers 3:15-39). They did the work of the temple, and they were 'paid' for their work by the other tribes.

Let's consider the nature of their work. There were many tasks that were not 'priestly', but necessary for the operation of the Tabernacle. The New Testament never implies that administration is unnecessary. To the contrary, Paul specifically wrote concerning 'setting in order' things that were amiss. I believe this consisted of both spiritual and operational matters (I Corinthians 11:34; Titus 1:5). The fact that administrative duties were not highlighted in scripture does not mean they did not exist. How else could you account for Luke knowing how many people were identified as 'being saved' at Pentecost, followed by another specific number of people 'being added' a short time later? This suggests that some records were being kept (Acts 2:41; Acts 4:4). If there were no records or bookkeeping required, how could Paul know his needs and the needs of his companions (Acts 20:34)? Judas was the treasurer for Jesus and the disciples. A treasurer, good or bad must maintain some record of the money (John 12:6; John 13:29). Some scholars believed that Paul dictated his letters, and someone else wrote and distributed them. Regarding the book of Colossians, F.F. Bruce made the following observation:

> On the point of authorship, Paul and Timothy are named together in the opening salutation as senders of the letter. It has been shown that most of the epistles in which Timothy's name is conjoined in this way with Paul's present some common literary features, which mark them off from other letters in the corpus Paulinum; a natural explanation of this would be that in these letters Timothy served the apostle as his amanuensis.[1]

For those not familiar with the term amanuensis (pronounce ah-man-yoo-entsis), it describes a person who is employed to write from dictation or to copy a manuscript. What F.F. Bruce said is that, although Timothy was Paul's son in the Gospel (2 Timothy 1:2), and a traveling companion, it seems plausible that Paul dictated his letters

---

[1] F.F Bruce *Paul: Apostle Of The Heart Set Free* © 1977 The Paternoster Press, Ltd. Page 408

and paid Timothy to transcribe them. Again, maybe this explains why Paul made it clear that he took care of himself and those who accompanied him (Acts 20:34).

In the Old Testament, we tend to emphasize the leadership of Moses, and give him credit for the Tabernacle. We rarely mention the workmen God anointed to erect and maintain it (Exodus 35:30-35). Much is said about Solomon building the temple, but little consideration is given to Hiram — a skilled, behind-the-scenes worker (1 Kings 7:13-14). Ezra, in the Old Testament, was a scribe, and the genealogical records in Matthew and Luke are a result of someone keeping records (Matthew 1:1-16; Luke 3:23-38). We have, inadvertently, placed so much value on apostles, prophets, and other ministry gifts that other behind-the-scenes workers have become the 'uncomely parts' of the body that, too often, are dishonored and overlooked (1 Corinthians 12:20-24).

There are many 'behind the scenes' duties that must be done. The optimum situation is to trust God to raise up those with the passion and skills for things like record keeping, bookkeeping, printing, and maintaining websites, etc. God can still fill men and women with ability to fulfill these needs. When their tasks exceed what can be done on a voluntary basis, then it would be in order to provide compensation to them.

## GIVING TO APOSTLES

Local ekklesia should receive offerings to assist itinerant apostles. Like all other offerings, this should be voluntary. There is no biblical evidence that apostles were on the 'payroll' of any local body, but it was

41

clear that believers gave financial support to their work. Paul addressed this issue with the Corinthians. He made it clear that if no one else recognized his input into their lives, they surely should (I Corinthians 9:1-2). He then reminds them that he too has the need to eat, drink, and maintain a family (vs. 3-4). Yet, it seemed that the Corinthians had left him and Barnabas to fend for themselves (vs. 6). This is a common fear I hear among contemporary apostles. This has led some to create 'apostolic networks' where giving is mandated. I have sadly noted that the 'big donors' in these networks are touted and honored by the 'leading apostle'; yet, the smaller givers are hardly recognized at all. This modern-day practice cannot be found implicitly or explicitly in scripture.

> If we have sown unto you spiritual things, is it a great thing if we shall reap your carnal things? If others be partakers of this power over you, are not we rather? Nevertheless we have not used this power; but suffer all things, lest we should hinder the gospel of Christ. (1Corithians 9:11-12)

Even though Paul poured his life into the Corinthian believers, he refused to demand that they support him. His primary motive was to further the gospel. However, to neglect financial support of apostles is as wrong as apostles placing demands for compensation.

Modern day apostles should take note of Paul's attitude.

> Receive us; we have wronged no man, we have corrupted no man, we have defrauded no man. (2Corithians 7:2)

> I robbed other [ekklesia] by receiving support from them so as to serve you. And when I was with you and needed something, I was not a burden to anyone, for the brothers who came from Macedonia supplied what I needed. I have kept myself from being a burden to you in any way, and will continue to do so. (2 Corinthians 11:8-9 NIV)

42

Behold, the third time I am ready to come to you; and I will not be burden-
some to you: for I seek not yours, but you: for the children ought not to
lay up for the parents, but the parents for the children. (2Corithians 12:14)

The challenge for us is to find ways to begin to funnel precious
resources into Kingdom advancing activities and purposes. The above
examples are not exhaustive, but serve to give us a glimpse of the priorities found in scripture.

## TRANSITION AREA 3: WE MUST TRANSITION FROM DENOMINATIONAL DOCTRINALISM TO EMBRACING THE VALUES OF THE KING

Man, in his attempt to understand God, has taken some of the truths
revealed to him and created the encampments we call denominations.
Truths that were intended to strengthen the Body of Christ became
lines of demarcation that encourage division. The high places torn
down by the prophets in the Old Testament have been replaced in this
day by sectarian beliefs.

In the first century, doctrine brought believers together. The only
thing that separated them was geography. I once heard it said that the
disciples were first called Christians in Antioch to distinguish them
from the world. Today we call ourselves Baptist, Methodists, Luther-
ans, Pentecostals and the like, to distinguish ourselves from each other.

In one city, there can be literally dozens, even hundreds of religious sects all claiming to serve the same God. Yet, each group shuns
the others solely based on their beliefs. This is not new. Among the
Corinthian believers, factions began to arise. Some followed Paul and
others followed Apollos or Peter. They were drawn to the teachings

of these men and seemed to feel that by following them they were somehow better than the other groups. That was the basis of the contentions among them. Paul dealt with their foolishness decisively( I Corinthians I:10-13).

First century believers embraced five basic values: I) the Lordship of Jesus Christ, 2) the priesthood of all believers, 3) the full expression of the Holy Spirit, 4) growing spiritually and expanding the Kingdom through covenant relationships, and 5) that no one among them would lack the resources they needed to fulfill their purpose in Christ. Apostolic doctrine brought clarity to these values. So, where ever you were, Corinth or Thessalonica, Rome or Ephesus, the values and the doctrines were basically the same. The ekklesia must be one.

## TRANSITION AREA 4: WE MUST TRANSITION FROM 'HUMANISTIC AND RELIGIOUS UNITY' TO 'ONENESS IN CHRIST'

I have attended many church 'fellowship' services. These are functions when two or more 'churches' come together to have a worship service. They pat each other on the back and declare that they are showing their community that the 'church' is unified. Although this is a good beginning, I differ as to whether it is a true example of unity.

First, not all 'churches' participate in these fellowship meetings. In the community where I live, there are over fifty 'churches'. We have a fifth Sunday fellowship service that is open to all of them, but less than twenty participate. There are as many reasons for not participating among those who are not involved, as there are unspoken motives for those who are.

44

Second, for about two hours every fifth Sunday, the participating churches will sing the same songs, smile at each other, and share the same finger sandwiches, cookies, coffee and punch. On a rotating basis, one of the pastors in the fellowship will bring the message for the evening. The two primary rules of the fellowship have been made clear: (1) the preaching pastor is not allowed to preach doctrine (specifically his own); and (2) the fifth Sunday is strictly for Christian fellowship.

On the surface this is admirable, but there is one little caveat that must be considered. The fact that preaching doctrine is forbidden does not mean that doctrinal biases aren't peppered into the most carefully structured messages. A scripture can be read and immediately it will be interpreted by the religious distinctions in the room.

Keep in mind that each 'church' represented, adheres to a set of doctrinal dogmas that many times conflict with the beliefs of another 'church' in the room. Some of the doctrines imply who is, or is not saved. So, the question must be asked, *'how can I 'fellowship' with someone whose doctrinal position denies that I am saved?'*

I and my Father are one. (John 10:30)

And now I am no more in the world, but these are in the world, and I come to thee. Holy Father, keep through thine own name those whom thou hast given me, that they may be one, as we are. (John 17:11)

And the glory which thou gavest me I have given them; that they may be one, even as we are one: I in them, and thou in me, that they may be made perfect in one; and that the world may know that thou hast sent me, and hast loved them, as thou hast loved me. (John 17:22-23)

Endeavouring to keep the unity (henotes) of the Spirit in the bond of peace. (Ephesians 4:3)

Till we all come in the <u>unity (henotes) of the faith</u>, and of the knowledge of the Son of God, unto a perfect man, unto the measure of the stature of the fulness of Christ: (Ephesians 4:13)

The principle in scripture is that we, the Body of Christ, be as one. We can only be one in Christ (Colossians 3:11). Jesus prayed that we would be one, even as He was One with the Father (John 17:22). We tend to focus more on humanistic unity, rather than becoming one. Let me explain.

The word *unity* in the above scriptures is translated from the Greek word *henotes*, that means 'oneness'. When Jesus said, "I and my Father are one", the Greek word translated as *one* is *heis*. Implicit in what He said was that He and His Father were *one and the same*. That is why the Jews sought to stone Him (John 5:18). What the contemporary 'church' often practices is *humanistic and religious unity* rather than unity [henotes] in the biblical sense. What is the difference between humanistic and religious unity and oneness?

In recent years, there has arisen a new term called 'frenemies'. These are known enemies who come together, usually for a common cause. This can be seen when our government partners with an enemy state to combat common enemy. Neither of the partnering governments changes their political posture against each other, but collectively realize that their individual survival depends upon defeating an enemy they both deem a threat. Thus, unity can bring together opposing factions for the sake of a common cause. Keep in mind that their focus is on their common enemy.

I am not implying that churches who gather for fellowship are enemies of each other. However, we cannot deny that each church brings their own doctrinal distinction to the fellowship table. This creates a subtle undercurrent that perpetuates division.

Oneness, on the other hand, requires submission. Oneness demands that we empty ourselves of personal ambition. *Oneness is focused on pleasing our Lord and King rather than defeating an enemy.* Our enemy trembles when we become one — first with Christ our Lord, then with each other. Powerful things happen when we become one. The Holy Spirit can fill and empower us (Acts 5:1-4); atmospheres can be changed (Acts 4:31); resources can meet every need (Acts 4:32-34); world systems will be able to see the risen Christ (John 17:21-23); all because we are walking as One Man — the fullness of the stature of Christ (Ephesians 4:11-13).

Many times, when church groups come together their rally cry is, "We will defeat the devil." NEWS FLASH! The devil was defeated two thousand years ago at Calvary (Colossians 2:14-15). Our adversary runs rampant in the earth only because we are so divided.

Think about it. Does a person who is starving to death give a hoot about whether you speak in tongues, baptize a certain way, pray in silence, or jump and shout? Does your pre-millennial, a-millennial, post-millennial, dispensational or Preterist eschatology impress a person who needs deliverance from drugs? Do those who are facing terminal illnesses concern themselves with whether they joined the right denomination? Sadly, there are those who read this that believe these things matter so much that, in their mind, it justifies their separation from other believers.

Our focus must change. We must set our eyes on Jesus Christ our Commander-In-Chief. We cannot truly see Jesus as the reigning Lord if we continue to idolize our belief systems. We must strive to be different from world systems rather than from each other. Jesus is not building a divided ekklesia. Church systems can be humanistically united, but the ekklesia must be one.

## TRANSITION AREA 5: WE MUST TRANSITION FROM 'CHURCH' TO EKKLESIA

Jesus never said He would build His 'church'. Based completely on the revelation that He is the Christ, Son of the Living God, He promised to build His Ekklesia. Yes, my friend, there is a difference between church and ekklesia. The entire concept of church was fabricated by man – not God. It's frightening to learn this because the ramifications are enormous. On the other hand, learning the truth is liberating and empowering to those who want to become what Jesus said we should be.

The next chapter will cover this in greater detail. Pray the Holy Spirit will open your eyes to see the glorious power that the Lord intended for you when, on the coast of Caesarea Philippi He declared, "…upon this Rock I will build my ekklesia, and the gates of Hades shall not prevail against it!"

...UPON THIS ROCK I WILL BUILD MY [EKKLESIA]; AND THE GATES OF [HADES] SHALL NOT PREVAIL AGAINST IT

JESUS CHRIST
MATTHEW 16:18

## CHAPTER 4: HOW EKKLESIA BECAME CHURCH

In the first three chapters I have regularly alluded to the fact that there is a difference between ekklesia and church. In this chapter, you will learn that difference. It will undoubtedly be the most critical part of this entire book for you.

In this chapter, I need to accomplish three specific things. First, you need to be convinced that ekklesia and church are completely different. Second, you will learn that the word *church* was substituted for ekklesia, and why the switch was made. Three, most importantly you need to see the impact this substitution has had on you and the Body of Christ. Please read this chapter prayerfully. Acknowledge whatever doubts, concerns, and questions you may have, and ask the Holy Spirit to guide you through this learning process (John 16:13).

49

## MATTHEW 16:18 IN NINE TRANSLATIONS

New International Version

And I tell you that you are Peter, and on this rock I will *build my church,* and the gates of Hades will not overcome it.

Revised Standard Version

And I tell you, you are Peter, and on this rock I will *build my church,* and the powers of death shall not prevail against it.

New American Standard Bible

"And I also say to you that you are Peter, and upon this rock I will *build My church;* and the gates of Hades shall not overpower it.

Bible in Basic English

And I say to you that you are Peter, and on this rock *will my church be based,* and the doors of hell will not overcome it.

American Standard Version

And I also say unto thee, that thou art Peter, and upon this rock I will *build my church;* and the gates of Hades shall not prevail against it.

Weymouth's New Testament

And I declare to you that you are Peter, and that upon this Rock I will *build my Church,* and the might of Hades shall not triumph over it.

Amplified Bible

And I tell you, you are Peter [Greek, *Petros* – a large piece of rock], and on this rock [Greek, petra – a huge rock like Gibraltar] I will *build my church,* (the powers of the infernal region) shall not overpower it [or be strong to its detriment or hold out against it].

World English Bible

I also tell you that you are Peter, and on this rock I will **build my assembly,** and the gates of Hades will not prevail against it.

King James Version

And I say also unto thee, That thou art Peter, and upon this rock I will *build my church;* and the gates of hell shall not prevail against it.

Nearly any translation of the bible you choose, Matthew 16:18 will record Jesus as declaring that He would *build His 'church'.* I checked over a dozen translations and only found two that used the word *assembly* instead of *church.* They were the World English Bible Translation, and The Emphasized New Testament[1]. There may be a few more, but I believe you get my point that the great majority of bible translations use *church.* I never questioned this, and I doubt that until now, you had either.

For those who like to dig a little deeper and investigate the original Greek words used in this passage, you will find *ekklesia* is the word that is often translated as *church.* Therefore, you can easily assume that *ekklesia* and *church* are the same. Again, we have been given no reason to explore this further. But just on whim, why not look up the word *church* in your own dictionary. Specifically, investigate its

---

[1] Kregel Publications. *The Emphasized New Testament* by Joseph Bryant Rotherham.

origin and the root word from which it is translated. See for yourself how it is defined, and if it is translated from the Greek word *ekklesia*.

In case you don't want to put this book down and do some research, I will give you two of the definitions I found. Take specific note of the origin of the word church.

## Merriam-Webster Dictionary

1 : a building for public and especially Christian worship

2 : the clergy or officialdom of a religious body

3 often capitalized : a body or organization of religious believers: as a : the whole body of Christians b : denomination <the Presbyterian church>c : congregation

4 : a public divine worship <goes to church every Sunday>

5 : the clerical profession <considered the church as a possible career>

## Origin of the word 'church' (entymology)

Middle English *chirche,* from Old English *cirice,* ultimately from Late Greek *kyriakon,* from Greek, neuter of *kyriakos* of the lord, from *kyrios* lord, master; akin to Sanskrit *śūra* hero, warrior


## Dictionary.com

1. a building for public Christian worship.

2. public worship of God or a religious service in such a building: *to attend church regularly.*

3. (*sometimes initial capital letter*) the whole body of Christian believers; Christendom.

4. (*sometimes initial capital letter*) any division of this body professing the same creed and acknowledging the same ecclesiastical authority; a Christian denomination: *the Methodist Church.*

5. that part of the whole Christian body, or of a particular denomination, belonging to the same city, country, nation, etc.

6. a body of Christians worshipping in a particular building or constituting one congregation: *She is a member of this church.*

7. ecclesiastical organization, power, and affairs, as distinguished from the state: *separation of church and state; The missionary went wherever the church sent him.*

8. the clergy and religious officials of a Christian denomination.

9. the Christian faith: *a return of intellectuals to the church.*

10. (*initial capital letter*) the Christian Church before the Reformation.

11. (*initial capital letter*) the Roman Catholic Church.

12. the clerical profession or calling: *After much study and contemplation, he was prepared to enter the church.*

13. a place of public worship of a non-Christian religion.

14. any non-Christian religious society, organization, or congregation: *the Jewish church.*

## Origin of the word church

before 900; Middle English *chir* (*i*) *che*, Old English *cir* (*i*) *ce* ≪ Greek *kȳri* (*a*) *kón* (*dôma*) the Lord's (house), neuter of *kȳriakós* of the master, equivalent to *kȳ ri* (*os*) master ( *kȳr* (*os*) power + *-ios* noun suffix) + *-akos,* variant of *-ikos* -ic; akin to Dutch *kerk,* German *Kirche,* Old Norse *kirkja.*

# Leaving Church Becoming Ekklesia

Using the Merriam-Webster Dictionary, and Dictionary.com you can see how 'church' is defined. But did you notice its origin? In neither dictionary do you find the Greek word ekklesia. Check most dictionaries and you won't find *ekklesia* there either. Why? Because, the word *church* is not translated from *ekklesia*. The actual root word for church is *kyriakon*. Jesus specifically said, "...upon this rock I will build my *ekklesia*" not *kyriakon aka church*.

The original languages of scripture all have the word ekklesia, yet it somehow became translated as church. The facts show us that church *is not* the proper translation of ekklesia. How did this happen? Was this a literary mistake? Is it just a matter of words evolving over time, as some have suggested? The answer is rooted in the history of both words.

I don't claim to be a biblical expert. I don't have a string of letters, Th.D, M.Div, or Ph.D, behind my name. I am just a believer, like you, with the ability to read and comprehend information. Many of the books I've read, many of the sermons and lectures I've listened to, and in nearly every bible translation I have, has implied that *ekklesia* is the word translated as *church* — but it just ain't so.

Whenever I am confronted with new information, it is my personal policy to research it to the best of my ability. It did not take much digging to uncover the facts behind this switch of words. Once again I challenge you to go online and google '*origin of the word church*'. I guarantee that you will find more information than you ever knew existed. Article after article will concur that *ekklesia* is not the *church* and vice-versa. I encourage you to do your own research. By doing so, you will be more convinced of the reality of the switch.

One of the startling revelations you will discover is why this change occurred. If you are not sitting down, you may want to take a seat before you read this next statement. *The word ekklesia was deliberately mistranslated by the authority of King James.* Let that sink in for a moment. The switch from *ekklesia* to *church*, was done on purpose. It was not an accident. *Ekklesia* is the original word, and should have been kept. At the very least it should have been translated as *an assembly or congregation*, but King James appeared to want every hint of its true meaning erased.

> ## Ekklesia is what Jesus said He would build

*Ekklesia* is what Jesus said He would build. In the original language of the New Testament, *ekklesia* is found in over one hundred scriptures. If you consider the Septuagint, the Greek translation of the Hebrew text, you will find ekklesia used many times in the Old Testament as well. Ekklesia is the right word and should have been kept, and church is the wrong translation, and should be discarded. *Church* is what King James inserted — not what Jesus said He would build. Because of King James willful switch, nearly every translation of the bible uses the incorrect word *church*.

On the surface, this may not seem like a big deal. However, as we explore the *ekklesia* and *church* in detail, you will discover the damage this word switch has done to the Body of Christ.

## WHO WAS KING JAMES?

To understand the reason behind this change, let's consider some historical facts about King James. Surely if there is a bible named after him, it would be wise to understand as much as possible about who he was.

From his own writings, it is he considered himself a god. For example, during a dispute over the marriage of one of his sons, he disbanded the parliament for their criticisms. He is quoted as saying,

> "Monarchy is the greatest thing on earth. <u>Kings are rightly called gods</u> since just like God they have power of life and death over all their subjects in all things. They are accountable to God only ... <u>so it is a crime for anyone to argue about what a king can do.</u>"[1]

This statement coincides with his publishing of two books, *The Divine Right of Kings* and *The True Law of Free Monarchies*. Both show the absolute godlike authority he felt he, and all kings had. His line of thinking was demonstrated when the Puritans attempted to challenge the hierarchal order of the Church of England. They had proposed the use of a presbytery, along with the bishops. King James angrily rebuked them. He saw this as an attempt to diminish his power in the church.[2] Remember, he felt as king that he had absolute power. His mindset is important to understand in relationship to the *ekklesia.*

Prior to commissioning what we know as The King James Version of the bible, he had made himself the head of the Church of

---

[1] http://www.greatsite.com/timeline-english-bible-history/king-james.html

[2] King James favored the system where the he could rule the church through bishops

56

England. From his encounter with the Puritans, he clearly wanted to maintain its top down hierarchal order. The mistranslation he ordered protected his interest.

## Ekklesia

This is a good point to get a better understanding of the word *ekklesia*.[1] It is a combination of two root words: *ek,* meaning *out from* and *kaleo,* which means *to call.* So, it is easy to conclude that *ekklesia* simply means *to be called out.*

Words have basic definitions, but are at times, defined by culture. For example, in 1916, if I were to have said that, "Robert has a cool house". Those around me would have believed that I was referring to the temperature of Robert's home. In 2016, my statement would be commonly understood as complementing the style and look of his home. The basic definition of cool has not changed. However, its use in contemporary culture has created a different understanding of it.

In his book, Ekklesia Rising, Dean Briggs wrote:

Some words have a clear cultural and/or historical context that greatly illuminates their meaning and usage. Ekklesia is such a word.[2]

It is only when you grasp historically how ekklesia was understood in the culture of Jesus day that you will be able to comprehend why King James purposely mistranslated it. Surface definitions of

---

[1] https://www.ecclesia.org/truth/ekklesia.html

[2] EKKLESIA RISING: *The Authority of Christ in Communities of Contending Prayer* © 2014 by Dean Briggs Published by Champion Press Page 108

ekklesia won't give you the context you need to transition from church.

In my book, *NO LONGER CHURCH AS USUAL*,[1] I wrote that the people in Jesus day understood the ekklesia to be an arm of the Roman government.[2] The Romans assimilated this concept into their culture from the Greeks. The ekklesia operated in public affairs long before the Romans decided to use it. Ekklesia was not a Christian term in those days.

What was so unique about ekklesia, and why did Jesus specifically use that particular word? Ekklesia had been practiced for hundreds of years. It was commonly understood by everyone. When the religious elite, government officials, or any average Joe on the street heard you mention the ekklesia, they understood it and its purpose. It wasn't simply a called-out assembly. It was much more than that. The ekklesia was a governing council that established policies, legislated, conferred or denied citizenship, and elected officials. The ekklesia had ruling powers. Don't let this fact escape you. It is the very basis for Jesus using this word.

When Jesus declared that He would build His ekklesia, He knew those around Him would understand the implications. Jesus surely knew that the ekklesia was a ruling and governing body. That is why He immediately outlined its' authority by giving it the keys of the

[1] NO LONGER CHURCH AS USUAL: *Restoring First Century Values and Structure to the 21st Century Church* Second Edition © 2013 T. Lemoss Kurtz

[2] Ibid Page 31 (at the time of publication, I equated ekklesia as being synonymous with church)

Kingdom of Heaven. He expected the authority His ekklesia to far exceed the authority of the earthly ekklesia. His ekklesia would be authorized to bind and loose on earth anything that was already bound and loosed in Heaven. The borders of the Kingdom of Heaven would expand into the hearts, homes, neighborhoods, cities and regions. The criteria for being included in His ekklesia was having a revelation that He was the Christ, Son of the Living God (Matthew 16:15-19).

Get this picture in your spirit. The ekklesia that Jesus said what He is building has authority to rule on earth from Heaven. The ekklesia Jesus is building is a divine ruling and governing body of believers to impact the earth from Heaven. 'Thy Kingdom come and Thy will be done…' is the mandate and rallying cry of the

> The ekklesia was a governing council that established policies, legislated, conferred or denied citizenship, and elected officials

Lord's ekklesia (Matthew 6:10). The Ekklesia has access to keys that unlock doors that have kept the masses in darkness. The Ekklesia, when necessary, is authorized to break down gates that keep people in bondage (Micah 2:13). The Ekklesia has authority and power to act.

The ekklesia that Jesus is building must be reactivated today. The first thing that must be addressed is the system that has contained the Lord's people. It is called the church. The ekklesia must break free of the church system. This transition will require access to heavens keys,

or maybe authorization to forcefully break down some gates. Therefore, it is critical that you be clear in your heart about what the ekklesia is and is not. It is not a passive called out group of people who get
together each week, sing kumbaya, eat cookies and punch and wait
for the rapture. It is a divinely called out, ruling, governing authority
that challenges the Gates of Hades at every opportunity.

## KING JAMES HAD AN AGENDA

I tend to believe the devil used King James to distort our understanding of our identity as the ekklesia. You act according to what you
think (Proverbs 23:7). Even with the best and most pious intentions,
if you think in terms of church, and all its trappings, you will never
rise above that mindset. When you better understand the ekklesia,
you will recognize the divine intent to empower you to impact your
family, your neighborhood, your city, your state, your nation and yes,
the world itself. In the ekklesia, you are only limited by the assignment
given to you by the Lord. As you learn more about King James, you
will understand why he was the perfect candidate to implement the
word change that has affected your spiritual life – without you knowing it – until now.

King James was well educated. Some historians say that he was
more of a scholar than warrior. This can also be documented by his
several writings. He understood the original languages of scripture,
and the word ekklesia, and its implications, most likely, did not escape

him. Think about it. When the Puritans suggested the use of a Presbytery[1], King James brutally rebuffed them purely because he saw this concept as a threat to his authority.

At the Hampton Court Conference in 1604 he was reported to have said, "No Bishops – No King!" He was completely vested in the hierarchal system in the Church of England, of which he was the self-appointed head. He controlled the church through the bishops. He supported them because he believed the Apostolic Succession of Bishops[2] reinforced The Divine Right of Kings.[3] This is the mindset King James had when he commissioned the now famous King James Version of the Bible.

The king gathered several scholars to tackle the task of translating the bible that would carry his name. He then gave them a list of fifteen instructions they had to use in the process. It was the third instruction that reveals his intent regarding the use of the word ekklesia. In his instructions, he wrote:

> The old ecclesiastical words to be kept; as the word church, not to be translated congregation, &c.[4]

---

[1] The Puritans believed the church should be governed by presbyters elected by the congregations, rather than bishops.

[2] The Apostolic Succession of Bishops is the belief that all bishops can be traced back to one of the original apostles.

[3] The Divine Right of Kings asserts that the monarchy is subject to no earthly authority.

[4] You can document this instruction by researching KING JAMES INSTRUCTIONS TO THE TRANSLATORS. This is the third of fifteen guidelines he gave them. http://www.kjvonly.org/other/kj_instructs.htm

In other words, he specifically told them to use the word *church* instead of correct the translation *ekklesia*. The translators obeyed him without question[1]. Why did he oppose the use of ekklesia? Go back and review his mindset. (1) He believed in The Divine Right of Kings. (2) He did not believe anyone had authority over a king. (3) He rebuffed the Puritans because they suggested a Presbytery, which would have shared the power over the Church of England. (4) He ruled the church through the bishops. These four reasons help to explain his instructions to the translators. When you consider that King James was well educated, and that he had a keen understanding of biblical language and history, this suggests that he knew the ekklesia could potentially threaten his authority, possibly more than the Puritans. Using the word *church* would effectively hide the truth from the masses.

So, what's in a name? Everybody saved and unsaved, young and old, rich or poor can tell you something about 'church'. It is deeply ingrained in our social and cultural psyche. This one word has established a religious culture that dominates how most people measure their spiritual identity. Because the word 'church' seems so harmless, some may be tempted to dismiss any arguments for ekklesia as chasing shadows. The word church was not new to King James. Like ekklesia, it had been around for centuries before he commanded it to be used. For that reason, I want to share with you the root word, and the other

---

[1] In Acts 19, ekklesia was translated as assembly. For them to have used the word church, would have implied the possibility of illegal churches. It appears Acts 19 had to be translated accurately to protect the agenda of King James.

words that have been translated as church. You will see how we have lived out these false definitions and have missed becoming the ekklesia Jesus said He would build.

Again, the word King James used to mistranslate *ekklesia* was *church*. Notice in his instructions to the translators he said, "The *old ecclesiastical words* to be kept..." This suggests that other words for ekklesia had been used prior to him commissioning his bible translation. Let's explore these *old ecclesiastical words* and their true historical meanings.

The Greek word *church* is translated from is *kyriakon*.[1] In Scotland *church* was known as *kirk*; in Germany, it was known *as kirche*; and to the Dutch, the word was *kerk*. Basically, it is defined as 'the lord's house'. I purposely did not capitalize the word 'lord', because of the confusion around what *lord* is being referenced. Some would suggest this is a reference to Jesus Christ, while others believe it is a reference to the sun god, Christo Helios, worshipped by the pagans.

It is important to note that kyriakon was primarily a 'house'. You can easily see the impact that this has had on us today? Church is most commonly identified as a building. If you ask most people to describe 'church' to you, they will most likely describe either a building they go to, or a sectarian group they belong to. Even those who say that the 'church' is called out believers, usually end up describing a group called out and into a building or denomination.

---

[1] Earliest use of the word church can be traced back to the 12th century.

Let's look at the pagan connection to the word church. Church is also translated from the Anglo-Saxon word Circe (pronounced *ser see*). In Greek mythology, Circe was the name of a goddess who was the daughter of the Sun God, Christos Helios. She supposedly had the power to turn men into swine. What makes this interesting is that many pagans worshipped Helios, including Constantine. This explains why he ordered the first day of the week, SUN day, as the day of worship for the 'church' (aka the lord's house). Even today, the clear majority of all 'churches' gather on Sunday with no thought as to why.[1]

The 'church world' is a far cry from the ekklesia. It promotes doctrinal insecurity, which accounts for the thousands of denominational sects. Most people identify more with their sectarian belief system than they do with Jesus Christ. The church world is a containment system, and denominations deepen the level of that containment. I often say that when a person tells me what denomination they identify with, they are revealing the perimeters of their belief.

> Knowing this first, that no prophecy of the scripture is of any private interpretation. (2Peter 1:20)

Before you get angry and throw this book across the room and send a posse to hunt me down, I want you to think about something. When you submit to a denomination, you submit to an established belief system. You are taught, explicitly and implicitly, that you must

---

[1] This book will not explore the arguments relating to contemporary Sabbath Day observances. My purpose is to reveal words that are translated as church.

measure everything by the beliefs of that denomination. This is often presented as *judging everything by the Word of God*. That statement most accurately means to *judge everything by our denominations interpretation of the Word of God*.

When you hear statements like, *"We don't believe that"* or *"We don't do that"*, you should first identify who 'we' is. Is 'we' the entirety of the Body of Christ, or is 'we' limited to those embracing a denominational interpretation of scripture? If it is the latter, then these statements may be an indication that you are connected with a belief system that may potentially limit your spiritual growth.

I believe sound doctrine is vital to the health of every believer. Transitioning from the church system into a functioning ekklesia will require clear doctrinal foundations. The first century apostles may have had different ministry disciplines, but generally their doctrine was the same. They all walked firmly in the same values: the Lordship of Jesus Christ, the priesthood of all believers, the full expression of the Holy Spirit, growing and expanding the kingdom through covenant relationships, and no one lacking the resources necessary to fulfill their purpose. From these values, doctrines were taught that brought clarity to the ekklesia in the first century.

To be free on the Lord's terms means you must first identify who and what is holding you captive. That is the dilemma we are in today. The transition from church to ekklesia can be a daunting undertaking. Generally, the religious masses have no clue that there is a difference between the two. Someone said that it took ten plagues to get Israel out of Egypt, but it took forty years to get Egypt out of Israel.

# Leaving Church Becoming Ekklesia

Many who read this will choose to remain 'church folks' and reject becoming the ekklesia simply because 'church' is the only thing they have ever known. They prefer the miserable comfort of the known, rather than the uneasy path to the unknown. Others will believe this is no big deal. "Why not just leave things the way they are?" Some will blatantly turn a blind eye to the undeniable, historical fact that there is a difference between what it means to be 'the ekklesia' against what they know of 'church'. Simultaneously, there will be many 'church leaders' giving glowing lip service to 'equipping the saints for the work of ministry' while defining the work as task that ultimately benefit the church system they know.

> The religious status quo has fought every major move of God since the Reformation

There will also be the heresy hunters. These are people who believe it is their duty to find error in anything they deem to be new. The religious status quo has fought every major move of God since the Reformation. Frankly, I believe they are an asset to the purposes of God. Why? For those of us who are navigating and pioneering new horizons, it is good to have your path tried and tested. Even Paul wisely submitted his revelation privately to 'those of reputation' so that he would not run in vain (Galatians 2:2). Likewise, the manuscript of this book was submitted to others who had full authority to challenge anything I have written.

I am keenly and deeply aware of my own shortcomings. The necessity to transition from church to ekklesia is fresh in my spirit. I don't pretend to have all the answers, but I am not afraid to fire a shot across the bow to alert the hearts of those in the 'church as we know it'. I write this book to challenge believers to begin moving in the right direction.

Recently, I taught a five-part series entitled *Understanding What Jesus Is Building*. In the first three sessions, I laid the groundwork for the heart of the series, which was the historical mistranslation of ekklesia into the word church. To my grateful surprise, by the time we got to the third session, many in the class had discovered the facts on their own. The class quickly shifted from gaining information to seeking instruction for activation. There was a divine impartation that swept the room, and several began to 'connect the dots' of things they had learned in the past to the reality of the present truth. Scripture they had heard and quoted for years took on new life as they grasped the purpose of the ekklesia, even on the surface. I pray that you will experience this level of impartation too.

## A WORD OF CAUTION

God imparts truth to draw us closer to Him. He imparts wisdom to strengthen us for His purpose. He releases fresh revelation to align us with His purposes. Yet, revelation can be dangerous in the wrong hands. Learning something new can become a fad for some, or a weapon for others.

As I studied, researched, and taught the material in this book, two serious and probing questions were brought to my attention. First, "If in our quest to discover the accurate wineskin, is it possible that the wine itself has been tainted?" Second, while teaching the class on ekklesia, one person asked, "If we have discovered that the word *church* was willfully mistranslated in our bibles, can we trust the rest of the bible to be accurate?" Both concerns must be addressed. First, lets' look at the potential tainting of the wine. This idea implies that the bible has been so corrupted by man, that it cannot be trusted.

> ## Only Truth can overcome lies or the misrepresentation of historical facts

The internet has opened a floodgate of ideas, theories and access to information at the click of a mouse. One tactic of the enemy in recent years is to twist historical information into propaganda intended to weaken and destroy Christianity. Yes, it is a fact that men have twisted scripture to justify many evil acts like the Crusades and slavery in the name of Christianity. It's a fact that some pagan concepts and ideas have been mixed into the 'church' culture. Some teach that the bible is a mythological tool used to control people. There are people teaching that Christianity is a copycat religion, plagiarizing stories written thousands of years before Christ. And now, in this book you are being introduced to the *church ekklesia* switcheroo.

These things cannot be ignored. Sticking your head in the religious or denominational sand won't make them go away. Only Truth can overcome lies or the misrepresentation of historical facts. Only Truth, not religious ideology, can bind the effect of dark and deadly theology on the minds and in the hearts of men and women. It is

Truth that reveals the heart of the Father for every generation. Truth is not just a book we call the Bible, Truth is Jesus Christ, the Living Word of God (John 1:1; 14:6; Revelation 19:13). He will build His ekklesia with those who have the revelation that He is the Christ, Son of the Living God.

Let me remind you of the premise of this book. We must transition from *church* to *ekklesia*. *Ekklesia* was mistranslated *church* at the instructions of a man, King James. *Ekklesia* is what Jesus said He would build, *church* is what King James substituted. *Ekklesia* was historically understood to be a ruling council. *Church* is generally a building filled with people. But beyond these contrast, we must take hold of what Jesus intended. He made it known that the ekklesia would overcome the Gates of Hades.

Hades is the abode of death. Dead people. Dead ideology. Dead philosophies. Dead religion and dead gods. It's within this realm of this dead underworld that antichristian ideas are birthed and vomited out into an unsuspecting and gullible world. The target becomes anyone who would give ear to their dark teachings.

> One tactic of the enemy in recent years is to twist historical information into propaganda intended to weaken and destroy Christianity

Their purpose is to foster fear, doubt and confusion in the earth, specifically within the ranks of Christendom. Truth sends light into dark places. Jesus Christ, the Living Word of God, exposes the thoughts and very intent of the heart (Hebrews 4:12). Thus, this is not a battle of philosophies and religion (flesh and blood) but an exposure of eternal intent to overcome darkness (Ephesians 3:10-11).

In these conflicts, we must realize that our warfare is not at the flesh and blood level. The enemy attempts to draw us into the fray at that level, because he knows that it would pit worldly intellectualism against spiritual truth. To the carnal mind, both secular or religious, the intellectual arguments would appear the most logical. Spiritual weaponry does not make sense to the carnal mind. The weapons we utilize are strategic in the spirit, and they must only be used at the instructions of the Holy Spirit. To the carnal mind our actions may seem futile, but in our obedience, they can:

- Open oceans with a rod (Exodus 14:16-21)

- Destroy impenetrable walls with a seven-day march (Joshua 6:1-20)

- Defeat massive armies with 300 men using trumpets and lanterns (Judges 7:16-25)

- Defeat trained gigantic warriors with a slingshot (1Samuel 17:47-51)

- Defeat massive armies with a choir (2Chronicles 20:20-23)

The greatest strategic move of the Father sent His Son to the cross, raised Him from the dead, and opened the way for billions of believers to carry out His will in the earth through Him (1Corinthians 26-8).

Some translators may have tainted the bible, but the Word of God remains pure. God is not intimidated by corruption. His Word will not be diminished by the nefarious actions of self-centered men (Psalms 119:140; Proverbs 30:5). Keep the original purpose of God in your heart. His intent from the beginning was to empower man to rule and manage the earth (Genesis 1:28; 2:15). Embracing the transition from the man-made church to the ekklesia, can empower you through the Holy Spirit. That is why this book was written. For we are not as the many, *corrupting the word of God*: but as of sincerity, but as of God, in the sight of God, speak we in Christ (2Corinthians 2:17 ASV). Pray over this book and everything you read outside of scripture. The Holy Spirit will help you to discern Truth from trickery.

This leads us to the second question, "If we have discovered that the word *church* was willfully mistranslated in our bibles, can we trust the rest of the bible to be accurate?" My answer is emphatically, "Yes!" The Word of God is true, even though men have tampered with it in an attempt to appease their political and personal agendas. The foundation of satan's deception in the Garden into this very day is to distort God's word.

> Now the serpent was more cunning than any beast of the field which the LORD God had made. And he said to the woman, "Has God indeed said, 'You shall not eat of every tree of the garden'?" And the woman said to the serpent, "We may eat the fruit of the trees of the garden; "but of the fruit of the tree which is in the midst of the garden, God has said, "You shall not eat it, nor shall you touch it, lest you die." (Genesis 3:1-3 NKJV)

This very first interaction between the woman and the serpent shows his intent to introduce doubt regarding God's Word. The woman knew God's instruction but allowed the devil to define it. The

71

result was devastating to all humanity (Romans 5:12). This could have been repeated in a hot Judean desert when the same devil tried to tempt Jesus after forty days of fasting.

> When He had been baptized, Jesus came up immediately from the water; and behold, the heavens were opened to Him, and He saw the Spirit of God descending like a dove and alighting upon Him. And suddenly <u>a voice came from heaven, saying, "This is My beloved Son, in whom I am well pleased."</u> (Matthew 3:16-17 NKJV)

Jesus was baptized in the Jordan river. Immediately, the heavens opened and a voice declared, *"This is my beloved Son..."* This was the last declaration Jesus heard from the Father before being driven into the wilderness by the Holy Spirit. The devil tried to use the same tactic he did with the woman in the Garden by casting doubt on the Word of God. *"If you are the Son of God..."* was meant to cause Jesus to question what God had spoken. Praise God, Jesus' answer struck directly to the core of satan's intent. *It is not on bread alone that man is to live, but on every word that comes from the mouth of God* (Matthew 4:4)[1]! This time the results were devastating to the devil (Romans 5:19; I John 3:8).

Jesus said that we are to live by every word that proceeds from the mouth of God. This begins with the written word. The logos. There are many translations of the written word; some good, some bad. Many are scholarly attempts to translate the original languages. Some are clearly interpretive translations that underscore a doctrinal

---

[1] Matthew 4:4 from the Twentieth Century New Testament Bible

persuasion. Others are just translations of a translation. And then there are groups that teach that the King James Bible is the only 'authorized' version for Christians. It would be a daunting task for most of us to track down every mistranslated word or phrase in all these different versions.

I believe it is the Holy Spirit who brings clarity to the Word of God (John 14:26; 16:13). Beginning with the sixteenth century reformation, the Holy Spirit has been restoring biblical truths to the Body of Christ. Salvation by grace through faith, holiness, water baptism, the present-day manifestation of the Holy Spirit, the active gifts of the Spirit, and the restoration of the five-fold ministry gifts have brought us to this place in history.

It is God's intent to release millions of believers into the earth to expand His kingdom. To do this, He is recalibrating religious structures, challenging hierarchal systems, and revealing to the saints their identity and purpose in Christ Jesus. The facts about the word ekklesia is not

> It is God's intent to release millions of believers into the earth to expand His kingdom

new information. It's meaning and history has always been available. It is however, what the Holy Spirit is highlighting in this season. I believe this falls under one of those divine truths *which in other generations was not given to the sons of men, but the revelation of it has now been made to his holy Apostles and prophets in the Spirit* (Ephesians 3:5).

We can trust the Word of God. The Word of God is strengthened by relationship. As you nurture your walk with the Lord, the Holy Spirit will release more and more to you. The information you are learning in this book is a tool to strengthen you. My prayer is that what you learn will provoke you to dig deeper into the Word of God. Only in His word will you find the foundation you need to pursue your destiny (Psalms 119:9).

Aren't you thankful that the Lord is opening your eyes to His purpose for you in this season? It is no accident that the facts surrounding the word *church* are being released now. God in His wisdom and timing gives us what we can handle. What He gives is accompanied with apostolic wisdom for implementation. That will be the focus of the remainder of this book. We will begin this next phase by looking at six factors that accompany a transition. Are you ready? Let's go.

He who shall introduce into public affairs the principles of primitive Christianity will change the face of the world.

Benjamin Franklin

## CHAPTER 5: SIX CHARACTERISTICS OF A MAJOR TRANSITION

Transitions just don't happen. Some are clear and obvious, while others are subtle and almost unnoticeable. A transition is the act of passing from one state or place to the next. A transition is the passage that connects a topic from the one that follows. It is a change from one form to another. With the latter, many people often miss or ignore the changes taking place and find themselves unprepared for the shift.

In Chapter 3, I outlined five transitions that I believe will take place over the next ten years. You don't have to be blindsided. This chapter will explore six characteristics that accompany transitions. These will eliminate the confusion that is created from what you see in the natural, and what you know in your spirit.

## I. THE OLD ORDER WILL STILL EXIST AND HAVE SEEM TO HAVE SIGNIFICANT POWER DURING A TRANSITION.

> And as they were going down to the end of the city, Samuel said to Saul, Bid the servant pass on before us, (and he passed on,) but stand thou still a while, that I may shew thee the word of God. Then Samuel took a vial of oil, and poured it upon his head, and kissed him, and said, Is it not because the LORD hath anointed thee to be captain over his inheritance? (1Samuel 9:27; 10:1)

> Then Samuel took the horn of oil, and anointed him in the midst of his brethren: and the Spirit of the LORD came upon David from that day forward. So Samuel rose up, and went to Ramah. But the Spirit of the LORD departed from Saul, and an evil spirit from the LORD troubled him. (1Samuel 16:13-14)

Israel wanted a king. They wanted to operate and be structured like the nations around them. It was not God's will for them, but He allowed them to have what they wanted. Their desire for a king was their rejection of God ruling over them (1Samuel 8:5-7).

First, notice that Samuel used a *vial* of oil to anoint Saul. A vial is essentially a shallow bowl or a flask. In either case, it is a man-made vessel. This typifies the kind of anointing Saul received. It was man-made. He was the people's choice, not God's. The people were taken in by Saul's appearance (1Samuel 16:7).

Second, it is interesting that when Samuel anointed Saul, he said that God had chosen him to be *captain, not king* over God's inheritance. Maybe this is just a play on words, but nevertheless, Samuel's choice of words should be considered.

76

The Hebrew word *nagiyd,* translated as captain suggests that Samuel saw Saul as a commander in front of the people, not the king. Captains were usually under the command of the king. They had authority, but their authority was limited to the king or pharaoh's orders. Isn't it amazing that the people wanted a king, and Samuel declared Saul to be a captain? I question whether the Israelites would have known the difference.

Saul proved himself to be a dismal failure. He regularly disobeyed God, acquiesced to the whims of the people, and had jealous and irrational temper tantrums. Even in one of his most grievous times of disobedience, his main concern was that Samuel would make him look honorable in front of the elders (1Samuel 15:30).

> The system of church that has contained, constrained and restrained believers is coming to an end

God rejected Saul; even though he seemingly remained in power, he was rejected by God. Samuel was commissioned by God to anoint a replacement (1Samuel 16:1).

This transition point is critical for you to understand. Samuel anointed David with a *horn of oil* in the presence of his father and brothers (1Samuel 16:1, 13-14). The horn from a ram or bull represented a sacrificed life necessary to carry the anointing. David's anointing for king, not captain, was not man-made. That is why what took place in the spirit realm must be understood.

77

The Spirit of the Lord came upon David and simultaneously the same Spirit left Saul.

In the heart of God, Saul was rejected. Yet, he remained in the role of captain/king over the people. God orchestrated the anointing of a new king while Saul was seemingly still in power.

David, God's choice, was not a 'ready-made' king, but rather a young shepherd boy who was not even considered qualified by his own father. This boy would spend several years in preparation for his role as king. Some estimate this process took thirteen years. Don't lose sight of the fact that during David's time of preparation, Saul was still in power.

## CHURCH BACK TO EKKLESIA

The church to ekklesia is such a transition. God has shifted his attention to His desire to have a fully functioning priesthood of believers (Exodus 19:6; I Peter 2:9). The system of church that has contained, constrained and restrained believers is coming to an end. It is the system that was put in place by man and has been allowed to flourish on its own strength for nearly 1,700 years. It is the institutional church. It is a carnal substitute of the ekklesia Jesus said He would build.

The institutional church is man-made and built on systems that use the Name of Jesus to glorify man. It is a system where iconic leaders are followed and where the larger the brick and mortar building is, the more successful they are considered. The

78

institutional church is measured by how many people attend a meeting rather than how effectively they expand the Kingdom.

We are in a world of mega-churches and pop-culture preachers. They won't be disappearing off the religious landscape soon. They appear to be strong, and their systems (according to worldly standards) appear to be successful. Those of us who are heralding a return to first century values and structure appear out of place. I believe we are like David. We have been anointed but must journey through our season of preparation until the day God fully restores and releases His Ekklesia.

In the meantime, has the Spirit of the Lord left the institutional church? I don't have a Word from the Lord on this. However, I will clearly say that His focus is His people, not their systems. Implicit in this transitional period is that God will allow the man-made systems to fend for themselves.

In this critical time, we must be careful how we respond and interact with those in the institutional church system. Why? Because most of us were saved in that system. Many of us got our spiritual foundations in the institutional church system. Then God granted us the ability to see something fresh from His heart. We have been graced to see His Ekklesia built His way. What we see is a privilege, not a right. Like David, we must handle what God is showing us wisely. David knew he was anointed to be king, but he behaved himself and acted wisely around Saul, who was still in power (1Samuel 18:5,14,30).

I am at times disheartened by those who attack the people who are in institutional churches. The people in these systems are not the 'bad guys'. They simply have not seen what God has shown some of us. Those who are attacked often entrench themselves deeper. David never attacked Saul, even though Saul sought to kill him. As far as David knew, God's anointing was still on Saul and he had no right to attack it, even when he had the opportunity (1Samuel 24:1-7).

I don't know what God will do with the institutional church system. All I know is that it is His desire to release an army of blood-washed believers into the earth who will turn the world upside down (Acts 17:6). In the meantime, don't lose sight of the fact, that for the time being, the institutional church system will appear strong and intact. Hold fast, God's time for His Ekklesia is soon (Habbakkuk 2:3; Galatians 4:1-2).

2. THE NEW ORDER WILL BE MARKED BY SUPERNATURAL MANIFESTATIONS AND PROTECTION

> And he said unto them, Go ye into all the world, and preach the gospel to every creature. He that believeth and is baptized shall be saved; but he that believeth not shall be damned. And these signs shall follow them that believe; In my name shall they cast out devils; they shall speak with new tongues; They shall take up serpents; and if they drink any deadly thing, it shall not hurt them; they shall lay hands on the sick, and they shall recover. So then after the Lord had spoken unto them, he was received up into heaven, and sat on the right hand of God. And they went forth, and preached every where,

> the Lord working with them, and confirming the word with signs following. Amen. (Mark 16:15-20)

The proclamation of the Gospel must be accompanied by the demonstration of power. Paul declared that the Gospel is the power of God for salvation (Romans 1:16). To the Corinthian church he said that he came to them in demonstration of the Spirit and in power (I Corinthians 2:1). Before Jesus ascended, He outlined the traits that would reveal those who were believers.

First, believers cast out devils. They dislodge demonic strongholds in individuals and territories and release the presence and power of the Lord in its place (Acts 5:16; 8:7; 19:19). Second, they speak with new tongues. This is not only the gift of tongues given by the Holy Ghost, but it is also the ability to articulate divine truth (Acts 2:4; 6:10; I Corinthians 2:13).

> And the seventy returned again with joy, saying, Lord, even the devils are subject unto us through thy name. And he said unto them, I beheld Satan as lightning fall from heaven. Behold, I give unto you power to tread on serpents and scorpions, and over all the power of the enemy: and nothing shall by any means hurt you. Notwithstanding in this rejoice not, that the spirits are subject unto you; but rather rejoice, because your names are written in heaven. (Luke 10:17-20)

Third, believers take up serpents. No, this is not the religious practice of handling snakes to prove one's faith. *Take up serpents* was translated from the Greek phrase *opheis arousing.* Jesus had already brought clarity to this earlier, when the seventy He had sent out returned. He revealed that He had seen satan (the serpent) fall like lightning from heaven. Then He told them that He

81

gives power to tread on serpents (demonic influences), scorpions (demonic attacks), and over ALL the power of the enemy. Isaiah prophetically wrote that when we go forth in the power of the word of God, the environment will respond in our behalf (Isaiah 55:8-13). Our rejoicing should not be in the fact that these forces will seemingly succumb to us, because the power is not ours. Instead, we rejoice because our names are written in heaven. We rejoice because we are in right relationship with the Father and His Son in the Kingdom.

Fourth, believers will not be harmed by drinking any deadly thing. Whenever you drink something poisonous, willfully or ignorantly, the results will be the same – death. Jesus said however that believers would not be harmed by drinking anything deadly. Let's look closely at who believers are, and what deadly things are.

> Put on therefore, <u>as the elect of God</u>, holy and beloved, bowels of mercies, kindness, humbleness of mind, meekness, longsuffering; (Colossians 3:12)

Paul exhorted the Colossian believers as to how they should walk holy and pleasing to God. Throughout his epistles, he frequently uses the word verb *pisteuo* and the adjective *pistos* to describe the followers of Christ. These two words describe the act of believing. The word *pistos* was translated one time in Paul's writing as *believers* (I Timothy 4:12), but it is abundantly clear in all the other uses that he was referring to the Body of Christ.

Nearly forty times he described the Christian community as saints. On four occasions, Paul used the word *eklektos*, the elect, to describe the saints. Jesus used the same word *eklektos* when describing events surrounding the end times. He said that it will not be possible to deceive the very elect (Matthew 24:24; Mark 13:22). I believe the elect and believers are the same.

When I was a new believer, I was given the impression that the 'very elect' were the 'very elite' of the church world. Implicitly I was led to believe that I was more likely to be deceived than the super preachers I saw in my denomination and on television. Whatever they said was usually unchallenged, because after all, they were the elect of God.

Thank God for His Word. It teaches that we – you and I, are the elect of God. The following scriptures apply to all believers, saints, and chosen of God.

> And the Lord said, Hear what the unjust judge saith. And <u>shall not God avenge his own elect</u>, which cry day and night unto him, though he bear long with them? I tell you that he will avenge them speedily. Nevertheless when the Son of man cometh, shall he find faith on the earth? (Luke 18:6-8)
>
> <u>Who shall lay any thing to the charge of God's elect</u>? It is God that justifieth. Who is he that condemneth? It is Christ that died, yea rather, that is risen again, who is even at the right hand of God, <u>who also maketh intercession for us</u> [the elect of God] (Romans 8:33-24)

Again, I say that the elect and the believers are one and the same. We have been blessed with all spiritual blessings and accepted in Christ Jesus (Ephesians 1:3-6). This is important to understanding why believers, God's elect, will not be harmed by drinking any deadly thing.

Deadly things are poison. I would suggest that Jesus was speaking metaphorically. Leaven is a clear example. Throughout His ministry, Jesus warned His followers not be taken in by the leaven of the Pharisees (Matthew 16:12). Leaven is not a liquid, but when a small amount is added to dough, it effects the whole lump (1Corinthians 5:6).

Also, like leaven being a type of the Pharisee's doctrine, I believe that the deadly drinks Jesus referred to could be a reference to false teachings and doctrines. Remember that Jesus warned us to watch for false prophets and false Christs (Matthew 24:24).

As it was during Jesus day, we are surrounded and inundated with false teachings in both the world and the church systems (1Timothy 4:1; Romans 16:18; 2Peter 2:1; Jude 1:4). These are the deadly drinks. Their doctrines have often become assimilated into mainstream Christianity, and some have been ignorantly embraced. Clearly one such poison has been the erroneous translation of ekklesia into church. Millions of believers fill the pews of 'churches' every week serving God the best they know how. Their souls aren't lost, but their impact is.

Jesus said that believers would not be harmed by drinking anything deadly. As believers become more aligned with the will of God, the Spirit of Discernment will begin to weed out demonic doctrines. This will result in believers/the elect, rejecting anything that does not line up with the Word of God. Deadly things will not harm them.

Finally, believers will lay hands on the sick and the sick will recover. Believers are ambassadors of the Kingdom of God. We carry the power of God where ever we go. We are empowered to bring healing to the lame, the blind, the deaf, the mute, the infirmed and any other disease satan tries to inflict upon people in the earth.

During this transition from church to ekklesia, there will be more and more manifestations of God's power. Healing and deliverance crusades will begin to wane, and signs and wonders will accompany everyday believers. The day of the spiritual icons is ending. More and more you will see them having to rely on their showmanship, while those who simply believe will do great works in the earth (Daniel 11:32; John 14:12).

## 3. THE LANGUAGE OF THE PAST WILL BE UNDERSTOOD BY THE PRESENT TRUTH REVELATION

I have found there are times when what is said, and what is heard can be miles apart. I will share this next part carefully because I do not wish to stir up old wounds or cast an accusing finger at anyone.

When I first began sharing the New Testament 'Church' model as I understood it – it was not eagerly embraced by some in our fellowship. There was resistance, specifically among some of the leaders, who eventually chose to leave. Unfortunately, there were a lot of harsh feelings and resentment generated on all sides of the issue. I felt justified in my anger towards the 'defectors' and I am sure they felt justified in their choices, too. These are good people that I believe love the Lord as much as I do.

It took the Holy Spirit to show me where I was wrong. He revealed that our disagreements were rooted in our language and what we understood the 'church' to be. We were saying the same words, but each of us had totally different definitions of what was being said. This was true in the first century, too.

> When they therefore were come together, they asked of him, say-ing, Lord, wilt thou at this time restore again the kingdom to Israel? (Acts 1:6)

Jesus had taught the principles of the Kingdom of God throughout His entire earthly ministry. For forty days after His resurrection, He taught things concerning the Kingdom of God. Now, just prior to His ascension, the disciples asked if He was going to restore the kingdom to Israel (Acts 1:2-6). What was the problem with this question?

When Jesus taught them about the Kingdom of Heaven, or the Kingdom of God, He was referring to a spiritual kingdom that manifests in the earth through believers (Luke 11:20). He taught them that the Kingdom was in them, not around them (Luke 17:21). He taught them to pray for the Kingdom to come on earth as it is in Heaven (Matthew 6:10). He gave them the keys of the Kingdom with the authority to bind and loose (Matthew 16:19). With all of this, the disciples main question was the restoration of an earthly Zionist kingdom that would throw off Roman oppression, and give the authority to Israel. Both Jesus and the disciples used the word 'kingdom', but how they defined it was totally different. Let's look at another example.

> Then Jephthah gathered together all the men of Gilead, and fought with Ephraim: and the men of Gilead smote Ephraim, because they said, Ye Gileadites are fugitives of Ephraim among the Ephraimites, and among the Manassites. And the Gileadites took the passages of Jordan before the Ephraimites: and it was so, that when those Ephraimites which were escaped said, Let me go over; that the men of Gilead said unto him, Art thou an Ephraimite? If he said, Nay; Then said they unto him, Say now Shibboleth: and he said Sibboleth: for he could not frame to pronounce it right. Then they took him, and slew him at the passages of Jordan: and there fell at that time of the Ephraimites forty and two thousand. (Judges 12:4-6)

One of the most interesting stories in the bible was when fugitives of Ephraim tried to cross over a critical point on the Jordan. Some apparently tried to sneak past the Gileadites. The Gileadites however had a simple test for those they suspected to be enemies. They would first ask if them if they were an Ephraimite. If the answer was no, they would ask them to say, Shibboleth. If the response was Sibboleth, the Ephraimite was exposed as an enemy and killed.

Their fate was sealed by their inability to pronounce the word Shibboleth. The bible says the reason they said it wrong is because, '*he could not frame* [his mouth] *to pronounce it right*'. Please understand this. In a time of transition from church to ekklesia, many will claim to be allies. However, the truth of what is in their heart is often revealed by what they can articulate (Luke 6:45). The fact that someone uses the same words that you do is not proof that they understand or support what you believe.

There are several words in the religious world that we have assumed their definitions for centuries. Some of these words are defined by our practices and folk theology, which are beliefs handed down that have not been tested by the Word of God.

I believe it was the differing definition of key words that created some of the conflicts I experienced. What I was saying, and what they were hearing became confused by our differing definitions. None of us recognized the source of the disconnect. None of us realized that we were disagreeing over a system that created division. Here is what I believe happened.

When I spoke of the 'New Testament Church', in my mind I saw a gathering of believers committed to the expansion of the Kingdom of God. The 'church' to me had become a living, organic force formed by the Hand of God Himself. I assumed most people would have agreed with this. I did not realize that I was seeing the ekklesia in my spirit, but still defined it erroneously as the church. I was trying to make changes to a system that was designed to be hierarchal, and that was a direct refutation to what I was seeing in my spirit – the ekklesia. I had absolutely no understanding of the ekklesia at that time. If I had, maybe some of our conflicts could have been avoided.

To most people, when you say 'church', they instinctively think of their denomination, a religious organization, or the building they go to each week. They verbally define the church in terms of a destination or a corporate entity. Some even speak of the church as being organic, but then describe it in context of an institutional operation. This opens a Pandora's Box of many other flawed definitions and concepts of the 'church'. Let's look at some of these communication flaws.

All believers say that Jesus is Lord over His 'Church'. Yet, how this is practiced can be confusing to an outsider looking in. On one side, they say Jesus is Lord, while at the same time they vote and politic for position and title within their *church* system. They create hierarchal caste systems that divides the *haves* from the *have nots*. The titles, authority, power and even the 'anointing' is primarily in the hands of the *haves*. The *have nots* are basically those who implicitly need the *haves* for their spiritual survival. It's funny that no one will openly admit to this, yet step back and look at most church systems and you will find that they are structured to sustain themselves this way.

On the other extreme, there is another more recent group who also declare that Jesus is Lord over His 'Church'. This group believes they only need to hear from Jesus, and that no human has the right to speak into their lives. They believe they are free to follow the 'Spirit' when and where ever 'He' leads them. This belief is often an overreaction of people who have been wounded and disillusioned by institutional church systems. It has created a disconnected cluster of isolated, lone wolf, and self-aggrandizing people.

Both groups say that Jesus is Lord, but their practices expose how they define their belief. In conversation, they would say the same thing and at the same time be critical of each other. I use the word 'church' as my primary example as all sides, without understanding, base their actions on the support of, or the antithesis to, the church system. Neither appear to have grasped the ekklesia. This false identity has fueled the misuse of many other 'religious words and doctrines' that are defined by church practices, causing greater division and conflict in the Body of Christ. Here are a few to consider.

What do you think of when you hear the word *salvation*? Are sinners saved by grace through faith, or is contingent upon other acts that will consummate their acceptance by God? What about the Holy Spirit? Are you automatically filled with the Spirit when you are saved, or is the infilling of the Holy Spirit an act after salvation? Do you have to speak in tongues as evidence you have the Baptism of the Holy Spirit?

What is your view of the five-fold ministry? Do they exist today? Are they hierarchal with the apostle being at the top, and the others placed somewhere beneath them? Are they divine functions that serve the Body of Christ from the bottom up? Are they specific people called to serve in this capacity, or can any believer serve in a five-fold role at will? How do you see elders? Are they just older men? Are they an elite group operating in the church? Are they just men? Can women be elders? What about the Bible?

Is it the infallible Word of God, or is it a good guide book for life?

All of the above questions are based on actual beliefs floating around the 'church' world. They find root in our understanding of the false notion of 'church'. By arguing beliefs in the church system, we are in effect arguing religious concepts on the wrong battlefield. It's like trying to play football on a basketball court. Church is an alternate universe that has no place in the Lord's ekklesia. By Truth alone, false beliefs will be exposed and the damage they do will be contained. The coming transition must build solely on Truth because a house divided will not stand (Mark 3:25; Ephesians 1:10).

The coming transition from church to ekklesia must bring clarity to our language. When practical theology overshadows religious rhetoric and when demonstration overrides cliché-ic proclamation, then the Body of Christ will draw closer to becoming ONE, as Jesus prayed it would be (John 17:21-23).

## 4. Leadership Roles Will Shift

In the coming transition, the current form of leadership will begin to reflect biblical patterns.

Leadership in the church for the past 1,700 years has been hierarchal. Hierarchy is not the biblical model. Hierarchy is the model of the Roman Catholic Church and the Church of England. It is the religious government King James sought to protect. This top down system has allowed an elite few to oversee the masses. Unbiblical titles were created and biblical roles were distorted to produce specific perimeters of authority. It can be confusing when you see deacons in one church system serve only in the capacity of aiding the Pastor, yet deacons in another church system rule all matters as a governing Board of Directors.

Most churches have a 'top/down' structure where leaders are locked into several tiers of authority, with the person or board of directors at the top having the most authority. Therefore, depending on the church system, ministers, if they are even recognized, are inserted in the place that most benefits the system. Too often, leaders hold titles without skill or character. The hierarchal model becomes the breeding ground for political infighting as individuals try to jockey their way to the top. I have seen people gain top leadership positions in churches through political manipulation and strategically placed financial donations.

The role of the Pastor has been the most utilized 'office' in the institutional church. Generally, the pastoral role is considered the primary leader, that in many cases acts as the CEO of the church. Our common church structure paradigm is the 'one pastor over one church model'. Yet the ekklesia was always governed by a team of elders. The concept of having a single 'pastor' would have been foreign concept to first century believers.

Leaders in the first century were first and foremost servants. They served in various ministry disciplines, but those capacities were specific functions. Titles were used and understood, but only served to identify the function. Paul admonished the Thessalonian saints to esteem those who were over them in the Lord for *their works sake,* not their titles (1 Thessalonians 5:12-13).

The leadership roles found in the New Testament are elders, deacons, apostles, prophets, evangelist, pastors and teachers. An apostle has a different function than an evangelist. A prophet has a different function than a pastor (Romans 12:6; 1 Corinthians 12:4, 28).

There are extremes on all sides. Some *house church* groups have focused solely on the function, and eliminated the titles altogether. On the other hand, many *churches* are filled with people who hold titles, but who are often void of the function that should accompany it.

Elders provide oversight and protection to the ekklesia. The nature of their role is *governmental.* The ekklesia must also grow and mature. To insure it does, the Lord Jesus Christ gave five gifts to His ekklesia — the apostle, the prophet, the evangelist, the pastor and the teacher — often referred to as the five-fold ministry gifts or the ascension gifts. They were given to bring the ekklesia to maturity; to the fullness of Christ Jesus (Ephesians 4:11-16). Their role is to *develop* the saints.

Both elders and five—fold ministers are leaders. However, the *nature* of their work is different. The nature of the Elders work is *governmental.* The nature of five-fold ministers work is *developmental.* Failure to understand the difference in the nature of their ministries, perpetuates the hierarchal and somewhat dysfunctional leadership model found in contemporary church systems.

The contemporary institutional church structure is predominately performance based. Most people attend weekly meetings and watch a performance of praise teams, dance troupes and preachers. Even though many churches are beginning to recognize the ministry of contemporary apostles and prophets, it has become a pattern to try and plug them into this dysfunctional model. This results in five-fold ministry gifts trying to function in a model different from what is seen in the New Testament.

> ...most people have no clue that the current church structure has no biblical foundation

We have made the five-fold ministry gifts governmental and hierarchal. We have created spiritual pecking orders that are completely unbiblical. Modern day leaders are plugged into a system that promotes and protects the leader, more than serving the people. The sad part is that most people have no clue that the current church structure has no biblical foundation.

When you understand the heart of God is to release the saints for the work of ministry, it will be easier for you to allow the current line between 'clergy' and 'laity' to disappear. This divide, that never existed in the first century is disappearing. The priesthood of all believers is beginning to evolve. This does not mean the eradication of leadership, instead it creates the restoration of leaders to God's original order and intent.

## Restoring Five-Fold Ministers

> And he gave some, apostles; and some, prophets; and some, evangelists; and some, pastors and teachers; <u>For the perfecting of the saints, for the work of the ministry,</u> for the edifying of the body of Christ: (Ephesians 4:11-12)

For several years, there has been an emphasis on the five-fold ministry gifts. In our hierarchal mindset, many have camped on these gifts and created versions of apostolic and prophetic ministries that cannot be supported by biblical text or historical evidence. The focus became the *office* of the apostle and the *office* of the prophet, rather than the *purpose* for these gifts. Ordination services for apostles began to resemble coronations for Pontiffs. Prophets began crisscrossing around the church world spewing glowing prophecies for gain.

Let me be clear, not every apostle or prophet serves unscrupulously. Most are sincere and have the best interest of their 'churches' in their hearts. Once again, the problem is the *system of church*. It is not structurally biblical. Paul wrote that Jesus gave the ministry gifts to '*perfect or mature the saints, for the work of ministry.*' There was never an intent for them to become iconic 'offices' that lord over the people (Matthew 20:25-26; I Peter 5:1-3). Leadership must begin to resemble the heart of the Lord Jesus Christ.

5. THE FLOW OF FINANCIAL RESOURCES IN THE OLD ORDER
   WILL BE CHALLENGED BY THE NEW ORDER

I have discussed this topic earlier. It is critical that you see how the transition in the flow of money will impact existing church systems.

Follow the money trail and you will find the reality fueling most church systems. In glowing language, we declare our purpose is winning the lost to Jesus Christ. But somehow, money becomes the best mechanism to accomplish this mandate.

You cannot attend a worship service in a traditional church setting and not expect them to collect an offering. It is always to 'further the ministry'. But what does that mean? It means, paying salaries, maintaining the building, paying utilities, financing programs, and events, and if anything is left, do missions and benevolent work. We have justified this as normal to the operation of the church. If funds are weak, we simply appeal to the congregants using a myriad of well placed, and strung together scripture to coerce them into digging a little deeper into their pockets.

If we are to follow the apostolic pattern that Paul used, it would totally eradicate our church financial systems today.

> There seem to have been three rules which guided his practice: (1) That he did not seek financial help for himself; (2) that he took no financial help to those to whom he preached; (3) that he did not administer local church funds.[1]

---

[1] Roland Allen MISSIONARY METHODS *St. Paul's Or Ours?* American Edition © 1962, World Dominion Press

Some quickly argue that the culture and times are radically different from the culture and times of Paul's ministry. However, we must then ask why is it so different? The answer is simple. *We have created* a system of church that is radically foreign to any example in scripture. To keep it alive, we must collect as many dollars as we can.

Over the years, I have outlined five values that are critical to the Body of Christ. The last of those values is that no one among us should lack, specifically the resources they need to accomplish God's purpose (Acts 4:34). Further, it is important that we care for the widows and destitute (I Timothy 5:16), and that we give freely to those who minister to us (Galatians 6:6; I Timothy 5:17). But nowhere do you find the ekklesia bogged down with the financial burdens many churches experience today.

Martin Luther's 95 Thesis challenged the Roman Catholic Church. Most people speak of the theological implication of his arguments. Without question, they were clearly important. But I would suggest that his challenge to the church regarding the way money was collected was as much a trigger that fueled the reformation as was the theological presuppositions he set forth.

By exposing the people to the truth of God's word, Luther

> *We have created* a system of church that is radically foreign to any example in scripture

unwittingly created both a theological *and* financial reformation.

97

Theologically, he biblically proved the Pope did not have the right to grant pardons in God's behalf. He preached the truth that salvation is by grace through faith in Christ Jesus. This truth eliminated the need to purchase indulgences, and drastically affecting the financial coffers of the church of that day. In fact, Luther challenged the Pope, (who was very wealthy) to spend his own money to build Saint Peter's Basilica.

The question must be asked, "If there had been no financial ramifications to Luther's 95 Thesis, would the reformation have had

> This transition will challenge the institutional church system of raising money

the same impact?" I am sure some would have disputed his theological stance, but I would suggest that the financial impact of his thesis fueled the greatest response from the religious powers. The 'money' issue is still the most common question today.

In the first century in Palestine, Christianity was a community of believers. Then Christianity moved to Greece and became a philosophy. Then it moved to Rome and became an institution. Then it moved to Europe and became a culture. And then it moved to America and became a business.

Several people have been credited with the above quote. Regardless as to who is responsible, it rings with a certain truism that cannot be ignored.

The business of church in America has weakened it to the point of near insignificance. As the church becomes the ekklesia, giving will shift from maintenance to mission; from staff salaries to sharing with the poor; from programs that entertain to purpose that expands the Kingdom. This transition will challenge the institutional church system of raising money. Some may attempt to discredit those who follow biblical patterns of giving. I believe the shift in the flow of financial resources will force the institutional church system to re-evaluate everything it does.

### 6. YOUR MIND WILL STILL JUDGE CURRENT OBSTACLES BY PREVIOUS SOLUTIONS

The greatest obstacle we will face in the coming transition will be the battle that will rage between our ears. Our ability to navigate through this season of transition will be how well we can remain focused without the usual religious points of reference.

> And the children of Israel said unto them, Would to God we had died by the hand of the LORD in the land of Egypt, when we sat by the flesh pots, and when we did eat bread to the full; for ye have brought us forth into this wilderness, to kill this whole assembly with hunger. (Exodus 16:3)

Israel had been freed from four hundred years of slavery. The first obstacle they faced proved that only their bodies were free, and that their minds were still held captive. It is a sad commentary on anyone who would rather die in bondage, rather than face the challenges of freedom.

You and I, and everyone who may read this book have been held in bondage to a religious system called 'the church' for nearly

1,700 years. Israel knew they were in bondage to Egypt. Yet today, most believers have no clue they are being held captive to a religious system. This makes the transition from church to ekklesia more difficult for some to comprehend.

The primary reason for this is that many have no clue there is a stark difference between ekklesia and church. They will go on doing their religious activities feeling no pressure to change. Some will understand the difference but choose to ignore it. Others will consider this some fringe teaching that must be refuted. They will fight any changes that will affect the religious status quo. There will be those who embrace the transition and begin the journey towards becoming the ekklesia rather than the church. However, because there is no clear map to guide them, some will stall and seek asylum in the religious systems they have known. This last point can be seen among many house church proponents who have gone back into the 'system' they claimed to have been freed from.

It bears repeating that (1) there is a difference between ekklesia and church; (2) that we are in the midst of a transition to become the ekklesia. and (3), that there is a path to become the Lord's ekklesia in the 21st century.

This journey must be completely guided by the Holy Spirit. For many this transition is completely unknown. They will continue to do 'church as usual' and develop more programs in an attempt to compensate for what they don't understand or fail to see. For other, the handwriting is clearly on the wall of their spirit. They sense an uncomfortableness in their hearts that will only be satisfied by divine truth. Prayerfully the contents of this book will point you towards the truth that only the Holy Spirit can ultimately reveal.

After forty years of wandering in the wilderness, Joshua led Israel into the land it had been promised. An interesting passage stood out to me as I read this account.

> <u>And they did eat of the old corn of the land</u> on the morrow after the passover, unleavened cakes, and parched corn in the selfsame day. And the manna ceased <u>on the morrow after they had eaten of the old corn of the land</u>; neither had the children of Israel manna any more; <u>but they did eat of the fruit of the land of Canaan that year</u>. (Joshua 5:11-12)

It appears that on their first days in the new land, that they ate the old corn, because the manna that had sustained them in the wilderness had stopped. What a picture of victory. Can you see it? They were in unfamiliar territory, and their first meal was the old corn of the new land. Ekklesia may be unfamiliar to us, but we can enjoy the old corn that had been planted by those who occupied the territory before us. The old corn for us is the fruit of the Lord's ekklesia cultivated by the first century believers. It is to experience the power given to a collective body of believers who can legislate heavens will on earth (Matthew 16:19). The old corn in the new land is to enjoy the freedom to pursue one's calling, purpose and ministry as they are led by the Holy Spirit. The old corn in the new land is to be energized and activated by divine direction, rather than being entertained by the trappings of traditional religious systems. My friend, it is much better to eat the old corn in the *right place* (ekklesia), rather than settle for any food in the *wrong place* (man-made religious systems).

Transition and change is coming to the church as we know it. You must decide how you will respond. Start today by measuring everything you know about 'church' with the Word of God. Allow the Holy Spirit to instruct you in bits and pieces. As your eyes are opened, walk in the truth you know and trust the Lord to help you navigate into your place in the ekklesia.

It makes no difference what we call
it, if we don't figure out how to live it
out in the earth

Don Coleman



## CHAPTER 6:   ACTIVATING EKKLESIA

I am thankful to be surrounded by great thinkers who not only motivate me, but also provide checks and balances to my ministry work. As
I have shared the heart of this book with some of them, they have in
turn shared it with others in my inner circle of confidants. From one
such interaction I received a challenge that captures the heart of what
the rest of this book is about. Don Coleman said this about understanding the difference between church and ekklesia. "It makes no difference what we call it, if we don't figure out how to live it out in the
earth".

How do we live out the words of Jesus Christ in the earth? How
do we become His ekklesia when all we have ever known is the man-

made church? How do we overcome religious fears, social biases, cultural norms and our own insecurities that have entombed us in a church world that should have never existed? How do we answer questions about ekklesia, when we know that our responses will be measured by the norms of church intellectualism? The answer to these questions will be the focus of the remaining chapters of this book. Understanding the need to transition from church to ekklesia is futile if there is no scriptural path to achieve it.

> ...to transition from church to ekklesia is futile if there is no scriptural path to achieve it

Undoubtedly, the transition to ekklesia is on foreign lands and uncharted waters for most believers. The very words of Jesus Christ feel out of place against what we have been taught to believe. Frankly, to my knowledge, very few people have addressed this issue, and I personally don't know of anyone trying to live it out in any meaningful way. What you will read going forward is a roadmap. This is where you must be prayerful and rely on the Holy Spirit to help you in this journey.

## FIRST, THINK RULING COUNCIL - NOT CHURCH

To begin, I encourage you to do a simple exercise. For the sake of grasping the difference between church and ekklesia in your spirit, let's define ekklesia in very simple terms. Let's simply call it, the *ruling council.* Say it out loud — *ruling council.* Say it again — *ruling council.*

You may want to say it several times. Now let's revisit what the ekklesia or *ruling council* is all about.

Remember, historically the ekklesia was a called-out body with the authority to establish policies, legislate, confer or deny citizenship, and elect officials. The ekklesia in the first century had authority. The ekklesia was governmental. This is what Jesus said He would build through those who have a revelation of who He is. The ekklesia today must recapture that authority in relationship to the Kingdom of God.

The ekklesia is authorized to administer the will of God in the earth. Therefore, by saying *ruling council* instead of church, it will capture the essence of Jesus' declaration in your understanding. Everywhere in the New Testament where you see the word *church*, I want you to replace it by saying *ruling council*. This will help you begin to see that the ekklesia is believers, specifically called out to be a *ruling council*. Here are a few examples.

> And I say also unto thee, That thou art Peter, and upon this rock I will build my [ruling council]; and the gates of [Hades] shall not prevail against it. (Matthew 16:18)

> And Saul was consenting unto his death. And at that time there was a great persecution against the [ruling council] which was at Jerusalem; and they were all scattered abroad throughout the regions of Judaea and Samaria, except the apostles. (Acts 8:1)

> For Paul had determined to sail by Ephesus, because he would not spend the time in Asia: for he hasted, if it were possible for him, to be at Jerusalem the day of Pentecost. And from Miletus he sent to Ephesus, and called the elders of the [ruling council]. (Acts 20:16-17)

105

The [*ruling councils*] of Asia salute you. Aquila and Priscilla salute you much in the Lord, with the [*ruling council*] that is in their house. (1Corinthians 16:19)

To the intent that now unto the principalities and powers in heavenly places might be known by the [*ruling council*] the manifold wisdom of God, (Ephesians 3:10)

Continue inserting *ruling council* for *church* throughout the New Testament. Each time you do, remember they are believers who are called out, and recall the authority entrusted to them as the Lords' ekklesia. Everyone I've encouraged to do this began to receive a clearer picture of the Lord's intent. I believe you will experience the same thing. That is the purpose of this simple exercise.

## BECOMING A RULING COUNCIL

And God hath set some in the [ruling council], first apostles, secondarily prophets, thirdly teachers, after that miracles, then gifts of healings, helps, governments, diversities of tongues. (1Corinthians 12:28)

For though we walk in the flesh, we do not war [execute the apostolate] after the flesh: (For the weapons of our warfare [apostolic career] are not carnal, but mighty through God to the pulling down [demolishing] of strong holds;[fortifications]) Casting down imaginations, and every high thing that exalteth itself against the knowledge of God, and bringing into captivity every thought to the obedience of Christ; And having in a readiness to revenge all disobedience, when your obedience is fulfilled (2Corinthians 10:3-6) [Definitions in brackets inserted for clarity]

To become a ruling council requires apostolic strategies. I Corinthians 12:28 states, that God set apostles first in the earthly ruling councils. Apostles first, secondarily prophets. This is not a hierarchal list, but rather an order of functions necessary to lead us.

In his book *DEVELOPING APOSTOLIC STRATEGY*, my friend Tim Taylor states:

> God designed these gifts for spiritual war, strategy and for building on a large scale. They are catalyst. I Corinthians 12:28 gives an order of their function. God make the apostolic gift to be first in function and the prophet second.[1]

One of the functions of an apostle is to help demolish wrong thinking. If your thoughts are dysfunctional, your actions will correspond with your thinking. Therefore, Paul taught that our weaponry is not in the realm of the flesh, but rather it comes through God with the capacity to pull down strongholds.

**If your thoughts are dysfunctional, your actions will correspond with your thinking**

The phrase '*to pulling down of strongholds*' is translated from the Greek words *pros kathairesis ochuroma*, which means to destroy fortifications. Where are these fortifications? They are in our mind. They are false images (imaginations) that distort our view of the Lord and His purposes. They are 'high things' (ungodly systems) that have elevated themselves against God's will. These must all be rooted out, pulled down, destroyed, and thrown down, so that we can begin building and planting according to divine patterns (Jeremiah 1:10).

---

[1] DEVELOPING APOSTOLIC STRATEGY *8 Keys to Projecting Power into Every Sphere of Society* © 2010 Tim Taylor Watchman Ministries International Renton WA

## DIVINE PATTERNS

Let's begin laying the foundation you need to transition from church to ekklesia. I recommend that you study this material in the remaining chapters with other believers in small groups. Such gatherings with other believers is a biblically sound New Testament practice. There will be those who want you to believe that you need to attend their 'church services', and that all this talk about ekklesia is of no value. The reality is that scripture reveals ample information about the ekklesia, and says absolutely nothing about 'church'. Jesus Christ is committed to building an ekklesia; a ruling council. He never said He would build a 'church. Nowhere is there a 'church service' recorded in scripture. The believers gathered from house to house to edify, exhort and comfort one another (Romans 16:3-5; Colossians 4:15). I encourage you to do the same.

Often when we consider divine patterns, our focus is on physical items that are types and shadows of God purposes. God gave Noah a specific pattern for building the ark (Genesis 6:13-16). The Ark of the Covenant was built according to God's specific instructions (Exodus 25:10-22). The Tabernacle was built according to a pattern given by God to Moses (Hebrews 8:5). Scripture also show there are times when God has given specific operational patterns that reflect divine intent. This can be seen in Numbers chapter four when God gave specific duties to the sons of Aaron, Kohath, Gershon, and Merari.

We can glean from the New Testament writers that there were patterns instituted by the apostles. Paul had things he established in all ruling councils (1Corinthians 4:17; 7:17). He spoke of his intent to *set things in order* upon his arrival in Corinth, and he instructed Titus to *set things in order* in Crete. The idea of *setting things in order* implies that there were specific patterns and directives that were being implemented.

I wanted to discover why there was such an explosive growth of believers in the first century. How did the message of redemption through Jesus Christ go viral in a time when communicating was so primitive?

> Fellowship became the mechanism that identified the believers in the Lord Jesus Christ from everyone else

We have the internet, Facebook, television, satellite radio, cell phones, Twitter, and so many other means to reach people. They relied on word of mouth, and letters carried between cities on foot.

There are several factors that played into this, not the least of which is the work of the Holy Spirit in the lives of the new believers. In searching for answers, I discovered a divinely inspired pattern that I believe was instrumental in establishing a working framework for the first ekklesia. It is found in the record of what took place in the early days following the outpouring of the Holy Spirit on the Day of Pentecost.

## ACTS 2:42 AN APOSTOLIC PATTERN

Immediately after the outpouring on the Day of Pentecost, the new believers began gathering from house to house (Acts 2:46). This natural activity set the stage for supernatural effectiveness. From the first house gatherings, we can glean patterns from the Word of God that

109

can help us today. In Acts 2:42, Luke outlines four things the first century believers did in the days following Pentecost. I believe the order of his list suggests an apostolic pattern that can help us make the transition from church to ekklesia.

> And they continued steadfastly in the apostles' doctrine and fellowship, and in breaking of bread, and in prayers.

There are four things the believers did as they gathered. (1) they continued steadfastly in the apostles' doctrine, (2) they fellowshipped, (3) they broke bread or dined with each other, and (4) they prayed. In this passage, the Greek word *kai,* that is translated as *and,* connects 'continuing steadfastly in the apostolic doctrine, to fellowship, the breaking of bread and to prayers. Although each part is separate and distinct, together they form a cohesive pattern. The order in which Luke listed these four activities suggests the importance of not emphasizing fellowship before apostolic doctrine, or doing prayers before breaking of bread. I don't believe the order of these actions is happenstance. Here's why.

Luke wrote the book of Acts approximately 30 years after the resurrection of Jesus Christ. He was a traveling companion of Paul (2Timothy 4:11). Because of his close interaction with Paul, I believe we can safely assume that Luke's writings were influenced by him.

Luke may have heard Paul teach that God set apostles in the ruling council *first* (1Corinthians 12:28). It was Paul who taught the ruling council at Ephesus that apostles and prophets were their foundation, and he listed the apostles *first* among the ministry gifts Jesus gave

110

(Ephesians 2:19-20; 4:11). Luke probably was familiar with Paul telling the Corinthian ekklesia to follow him as he followed Christ (1 Corinthians 11:1). So, it should be of no surprise that when Luke described the response of the three thousand new believers to the gospel, it began with them 'following steadfastly in the apostle's doctrine' *first* (Acts 2:42).

The remarkable events that took place that Pentecost morning would have been confusing, had it not been for the clarity brought by the apostles. Remember Peter, an apostle, was the *first* to clarify the events when he explained to the crowd, "This is that which was spoken by the Prophet Joel…" (Acts 2:16). Apostolic elucidation took place first. It made sense of a whirlwind of new spiritual activity. It was not the limiting apostolic theology we have today that primarily emphasizes ministry offices or baptism methodologies. The apostle's doctrine was a comprehensive understanding of salvation by grace through faith, and empowerment by the Holy Spirit. It was in this doctrine that the believers remained steadfast.

Second on Luke's list was fellowship. Fellowship became the mechanism that identified the believers in the Lord Jesus Christ from everyone else. Three thousand had been baptized in His name, and then became a support system of sorts for each other. It was a heart felt kind of fellowship. It was koinonia at its best. This body of believers got to know and encourage each other so much that within a few weeks another five thousand more had joined them (Acts 4:4). The fellowship was so prevalent that Luke reported that they gathered in one accord in the temple daily and from house to house (Acts 2:46).

Third, fellowship became easily interwoven with breaking bread. This reveals the level of personal investment they had in each other.

Preparing a meal in the first century was not a '*run to the store – pick up a few items – throw them in the microwave – and serve*' type of event. In those days, if you were serving meat, an animal had to be butchered, dressed, and prepared. Vegetables had to be retrieved, washed then grilled or boiled. Breads required kneading and preparing from raw grain. By the time you sat down to eat, several hours would have passed. Breaking of bread required time and physical investment. These first three acts, the apostle doctrine, fellowship and breaking bread laid the foundation for the final piece – prayer.

The fact that prayer is listed last does not imply that it is the least important. I believe that prayer is the most critical aspect of our walk with Christ and with each other. However, it is vitally important that we are 'one' with each other when we pray. How can two walk together unless they have agreed (Amos 3:3)? Jesus said that, "…when two agree (first), as touching anything they shall ask, it shall be done…(Matthew 18:19). Paul encouraged the Corinthian believers to "…speak the same thing, and that there be no divisions among [them]; [and that they should] be perfectly joined together in the same mind and in the same judgment (1Corinthians 1:10). This level of agreement is birthed out of relationships that are nurtured from fellowship in Christ, and each other (1John 1:7).

Clarity of God's purpose outlined by apostolic doctrine, combined with fellowship and breaking of bread, creates the deep level relationships that are vital when believers come together to pray. They can lift their voices in one accord and expect dramatic outcomes in Jesus Name (Acts 4:24-37).

Why is Acts 2:42 important? Just as the three thousand believers on the Day of Pentecost discovered a new way to God through Jesus Christ, we have discovered that God never intended to contain us in a man-made system called church. Those first converts steadfastly followed clear, apostolic doctrine that provided clarity of purpose. They shared what they were learning among themselves through fellowship and breaking bread from house to house. Then they prayed, received wisdom from the Holy Spirit and in a short time, their numbers were more than doubled.

Acts 2:42 can serve as a template in your quest to leave church to become a fully functioning *ekklesia/ruling council*. The first chapters of this book showed you the difference between church and what Jesus said He would build. The remaining chapters of this book can serve as *apostolic doctrine* for this transition. Many times, during a season of transition, you must unlearn wrong beliefs to embrace what is scripturally accurate. You will discover what the bible says, and how Jesus fully intended to empower His ekklesia to bind, loose and challenge the gates of Hades. It is important that you *continue steadfast* in apostolic doctrine.

Like the first century believers, you should seek to fellowship and break bread with other believers who want to make this transition. Gathering in homes is the most biblically sound way to fellowship. We have been taught by tradition that fellowship is '*going to church*', hearing a sermon, paying our money and going home. Gathering from

113

house to house is an entirely different paradigm and may be awkward for some. Therefore, I have included a simple guide gleaned from the experiences of the gatherings we have both hosted and attended (See Appendix A). Your ability to impact your family, your neighborhood, your city, state, country, and even the world begins when you gather with other believers for the sole purpose of expanding the Kingdom of God in the earth.

Finally, pray. You and those you gather with should pray for wisdom and understanding. Seek the Lord for clarity to know more than *what* this transition is, but also *why* it is important to you and the Body of Christ.

Pray for direction. What will you do with this revelation? How does God intend for you to live it out in your community? How do you effectively share this with others? And finally, seek the Lord for Kingdom expanding strategies. Where does God need you to make a difference?

Allow the Holy Spirit to recalibrate you, and to align you more closely to the Word of God. Discuss this with those gathering with you. Encourage and exhort each other (Romans 15:14). Pray with and for each other as you, individually and corporately, navigate through these considerations.

Now, let's consider a contemporary definition of ekklesia.

There is no way around it: the Greek word ekklesia means something more and different than the English word church. The gap is meaningful and real

Dean Briggs
Author of Ekklesia Rising

## CHAPTER 7:   DEFINING EKKLESIA

How do we define the ekklesia in contemporary language? Yes, it is a ruling council. Saying ruling council rather than church gives us a basic working definition. However, is there a more comprehensive definition that describes both its meaning and function in the earth? This chapter will address this in detail.

In my book, *NO LONGER CHURCH AS USUAL,* I gave an extensive definition of the New Testament Church. When I wrote it, I believed that church and ekklesia were synonymous. In this book, I am adjusting the definition to reflect what Jesus said He was building – the ekklesia.

Throughout the remainder of this book I will use ekklesia and ruling council interchangeably. They are the same thing. We have believed that we are the 'church' for so that it is necessary to regularly define and clarify the ekklesia or ruling council. Defining the ekklesia or ruling council in practical terms can help you embrace what Jesus Christ said He would build. There are eight points in the definition that follows that will help you visualize the purpose of any ekklesia.

> The Ekklesia is an assembly of called out believers, committed to the Kingdom Mandate; who gather one or more times each week under the Headship of Jesus Christ; who are submitted to each other in love; who support each other's on-going work of being and making disciples of the Lord Jesus Christ; who edify, exhort and comfort one another; who submit and relate to elders, ministry gifts and apostolic leaders; who participate in planting and supporting new assemblies of believers to do the same with their prayers, time, finances, and material resources.

(1) **The Ekklesia is an assembly of called out believers.** The ekklesia specifically consists of *believers* who are called out to become a ruling council. Jesus is not building with unbelievers. He is building with believers who have a revelation of Him as the Christ, Son of the Living God (Matthew 16:18).

The ekklesia models the values, principles, and practices that were taught and demonstrated by Jesus Christ and the founding apostles in the first century. The New Testament books are a record of these pioneers living out their revelation of Jesus Christ through Old Testament text. The New Testament books we have today did not exist during their lifetime.

This called out assembly of believers were committed to implementing the purposes of the Lord Jesus Christ in the earth.

One of the first acts of the ekklesia Jesus is building is to confront the gates of Hades. This powerful ruling council is entrusted with the keys of the Kingdom of Heaven. It can bind and loose, declare what is legal and unlawful on earth from whatever has been declared as such in heaven. Therefore, it is inconceivable that unbelievers would be entrusted with this task.

(2) **Committed to the Kingdom Mandate** The Kingdom Mandate reveals God's mission for His ekklesia. The first command God gave man was to be fruitful, to multiply and replenish the earth, and subdue it (Genesis 1:28). Jesus reiterated that command when He told His followers to "go into all the world and make disciples of all nations" (Matthew 28:19). This highlights the authority given to the ekklesia as a ruling council.

Remember, the ekklesia in the first century was known as a ruling governmental council with authority to establish policies, legislate, confer or deny citizenship, and to elect officials. The ekklesia that Jesus is building has been given the keys of the Kingdom of Heaven with the authority to declare lawful or unlawful on earth, anything that has been declared lawful or unlawful in heaven. The ruling council represents the Kingdom of God in the earth.

The Kingdom Mandate is the sole mission of the ekklesia. It is the mission God had in mind from the foundation of the world (Ephesians 3:10-11). The ekklesia Jesus is building has been commissioned to challenge the Gates of Hades so that the kingdoms of this world will become the Kingdom of our God and of His Christ.

The ekklesia must continually and systematically recapture the territory stolen by the devil. The Kingdoms of religion, government, entertainment, media, business, education, and family must be regained and made subject to the Lord (Revelation 11:15). Therefore, every ruling council or ekklesia must be fully committed to the Kingdom Mandate and its completion in the earth.

(3) **Who gather one or more times each week under the Headship of Jesus Christ** Once again, it must be stressed that every ekklesia gathers under the headship of Jesus Christ. God made Him to be head over the ruling councils He builds (Ephesians 1:22; Colossians 1:18). Individually and collectively they function with the real revelation of Jesus as Lord and Christ (Acts 2:36).

In chapter six, I shared a pattern found in Acts 2:42 where the believers continued steadfastly in the apostle's doctrine, in fellowship, in breaking bread and prayers. What is more interesting is that the believers at that time met *daily* in the temple and from house to house (Acts 2:46; 5:42).

118

The Acts 2:42 pattern, and regular and consistent gatherings will be necessary for building strong ruling councils. I recommend having weekly fellowships and breaking of bread, where apostolic doctrine is shared. This will help lay the foundation necessary to impact families, neighborhoods, cities, states, and the like.

(4) **Who are submitted to each other in love**    Jesus said that the identifying factor for His disciples is the love they have for one another (John 13:35). There are more than fifty scriptures that address the interaction we should have with each another. Of all the 'one-anothers' in scripture, the command to love one another is the most prevalent. As we submit to each other in love, it creates an atmosphere for the Holy Spirit to work.

> Beloved, if God so loved us, we ought also to love one another. No man hath seen God at any time. If we love one another, God dwelleth in us, and his love is perfected in us. (1John 4:11-12)
>
> Herein is our love made perfect, that we may have boldness in the day of judgment: because as he is, so are we in this world. There is no fear in love; but perfect love casteth out fear: because fear hath torment. He that feareth is not made perfect in love. (1John 4:17-18)

In his epistles, John describes a love that is perfected. The Greek word from which *perfected* is translated throughout these scriptures is the verb *teleioo*, which means *to bring to*

119

*an end by completing.* What John wrote is that love is brought to completion through our interaction with each other. If we love one another, God's love is brought to completion in us. To paraphrase verse 17, John says, "This is how our love is completed". He goes on to say that, this complete love eradicates fear, and that fear is proof that we are not yet completed in love. All of this is predicated by our relationships with our brothers and sisters (I John 4:7).

This complete fearless love can only exist among believers who are in covenant relationship with each other. This by no means is to imply that believers are without faults. It simply means that a love that is being completed in one believer can find fellowship with other believers without being condemning or judgmental (I Peter 4:8). The close relationship that is nurtured through fellowship and breaking bread can serve to break down barriers.

(5) **Who support each other's on-going work of being and making disciples of the Lord Jesus Christ** There is no room in the ekklesia for anyone who does not give up all to be a disciple of the Lord Jesus Christ. Anyone who fails to do so cannot be His disciple (Luke 14:33). The price for being a disciple is high.

Jesus says we are to make disciples of nations (Matthew 28:19). This may seem like a daunting task, but Jesus Christ sent the Holy Spirit to help us. It begins at the personal level.

120

And I myself also am persuaded of you, my brethren, that ye also are full of goodness, filled with all knowledge, able also to admonish one another. (Romans 15:14)

And let us consider one another to provoke unto love and to good works: Not forsaking the assembling of ourselves together, as the manner of some is; but exhorting one another: and so much the more, as ye see the day approaching. (Hebrews 10:24-25)

Paul wrote to the Roman Christians that they had the ability to admonish one another. In Hebrews, the author encouraged the believers to provoke one another to good works and to exhort each other when they regularly assembled (Hebrews 10:24-25). This exposes one of the supernatural internal strengths of the ekklesia. It is during personal face-to-face interaction that believers are encouraged and strengthened. Believers in the ekklesia learn to bear one another's burden to the point of feeling each other's pain, embracing one another's sorrows, and sharing each other's joys (1Corinthians 12:25-26). This is how disciples are developed on a personal level.

We disciple Nations through the proactive prayer and Spirit-led actions of the ekklesia. These tight knit gatherings can become powerful ruling councils that are strategically positioned to address local, regional, statewide, and even global issues. Whether they pray to break ungodly alliances or create programs that address local needs, the ruling councils can disciple communities, cities, counties, and more. As ruling councils are formed, the influence of the Kingdom of God will expand in the earth.

If you recall, prayer was the last thing listed in the Acts 2:42 pattern. A fellowship of believers who have embraced each other in strong covenant relationship are more poised to pray and act 'as one' local body (Acts 4:31-32). As such, the gates of Hades will relent and the footprint of the Kingdom of God will be established. (1Corinthians 15:25; Ephesians 1:22-23)

(6) **Who edify, exhort and comfort one another**  Spiritual warfare is difficult. War is accompanied by pain, loss and casualties. Those in the battle can grow weary and discouraged. Even the apostle Paul spoke of becoming so burdened that he and his companions despaired of life. But he rejoiced that the prayers of the believers in Corinth had helped them (2Corinthians 1:8-11). Peter was locked in prison facing imminent death. But it was the prayers of the ekklesia that helped secure his release with angelic intervention (Acts 12:5-10).

We are called to edify each other (Romans 14:19), exhort one another (Hebrews 10:25), and to comfort one another (1Thessalonians 4:18; 5:11). Edification, exhortation, and comforting are all attributes of prophecy (1Corinthians 14:3). Prophecy edifies or builds, the ruling councils. When believers prophesy to each other, it brings strength to the ekklesia. It builds a spiritual camaraderie that can endure tough times and difficult situations. As New Testament believers, we must strive to create an atmosphere that will continually build those with whom we are in covenant with. This will keep the ruling councils strong.

(7) **Who submit and relate to elders, ministry gifts and apostolic leaders** Earthly leaders, who govern and develop the ekklesia, are under the authority of Jesus Christ. They serve from the bottom up, not from any top-down hierarchal position. Biblical submission is designed for protection. It provides a safe atmosphere to flourish for those who submit. It should be voluntary, because it ceases to be submission and becomes control whenever it is forced. We need not fear biblical submission.

To understand submission, you need to understand the leadership Jesus has set in His ekklesia.

> Wherefore he saith, When he ascended up on high, he led captivity captive, <u>and gave gifts unto men</u>. (Now that he ascended, what is it but that he also descended first into the lower parts of the earth? He that descended is the same also that ascended up far above all heavens, that he might fill all things.) And he gave some, apostles; and some, prophets; and some, evangelists; and some, pastors and teachers; <u>For the perfecting of the saints, for the work of the ministry, for the edifying of the body of Christ</u>: (Ephesians 4:8-12)

The apostles, prophets, evangelist, pastors, and teachers were given for equipping the saints for the work of ministry. Although the saints make up the ekklesia, you should note that when Jesus gave these gifts, He gave them to men or human beings[1]. Their function was to equip the saints for the work of ministry, which in turn would build up the Body of Christ.

> ... but speaking truth in love, we may <u>grow up in all things into him</u>, who is the head, Christ; from whom all the body, being fitted and knit together through that which every joint supplies, <u>according to the working in measure of each individual part</u>, **makes the body increase to the building up of itself in love.** (Ephesians 4:15-16 World English Bible)

Equipped saints must first grow up in all things into Christ. They become a body, joined together in which everyone contributes. Growing up in Christ must be first. The ekklesia is built from those who have a revelation of Jesus as the Christ, Son of the Living God. Ministry gift leaders help to guide believers towards that revelation, but recognize it only comes through the Holy Spirit (Matthew 16:17; I Corinthians 12:3). They strive to prepare the saints for the work of ministry. They help them identify their 'part' in the Body of Christ.

Dr. Greg Ogden detailed the process of equipping the saints in his book Unfinished Business[2] He breaks down this work into three categories: (1) mend/restore, (2) establish/lay foundations, and (3) prepare/train. He wrote that Paul defined equipping in terms of results.

---

[1] The word *men* in Ephesians 4:8 is translated from the Greek word *Anthropos* which means human being.

[2] Dr. Greg Ogden UNFINISHED BUSINESS: *Returning The Ministry To The People Of God* © 1990, 2003 Published by Zondervan, Pages 130 – 155

> Paul appears to define equipping, not in terms of pastoral images or functions..., but in terms of results. In other words, equipping is a means to a greater end. Paul is concerned that equipping ministry produce a certain product. We know that equipping is occurring if the saints are doing the work of ministry, the body of Christ is being built up, the whole body is attaining a unity of faith, and the community together is expressing the full stature of Christ. Or to put it negatively, equipping is happening if people are no longer children in the faith who are so impressionable that the latest "wind of doctrine" leads them astray.

It is the equipped saints that are more likely to have a revelation of Jesus as the Christ, making them available and capable to serve in the Lord's ekklesia.

Ruling councils are governed by elders. Elders were ordained in every ekklesia (Acts 14:23)[3]. Elders clearly governed the local ekklesia (Acts 15:4; 15:22; 20:17; James 5:4). Paul instructed Titus to ordain elders in every city (Titus 1:5). He gave instructions to the elders of Ephesus regarding the ekklesia they oversaw (Acts 20:17). And Peter exhorted the elders to feed the flock and to be examples before them (1Peter 5:1-3).

Leadership who serve the ekklesia as Jesus and the apostles, carry the responsibility of having others submit to them. However, true leaders recognize the responsibility they have. They know that every believer, including themselves, must

---

[3] This was most likely the collective ekklesia in every city, and not each individual house gathering.

submit to someone. (Romans 12:10; 13:1; Ephesians 5:21; IPeter 5:5). The basic function of the elders is to provide a safe atmosphere for the ekklesia to function and grow.

The concern of a Godly leader is to see believers fulfill their individual callings more than exalting their own perceived authority. They carry in their hearts the purposes of the Father, and the well-being of those who submit to them. It is not difficult or grievous to obey Godly elders and ministry gifts.

> Obey them that have the rule over you, and submit yourselves: for they watch for your souls, as they that must give account, that they may do it with joy, and not with grief: for that is unprofitable for you. (Hebrews 13:17)

The word *obey* in the above passage is translated from the Greek word *peitho*. It has the implication of one having confidence in another. Submission to leadership is easier when the leaders uphold the standards of scripture and our King, Jesus Christ.

(8) **Who participate in planting and supporting new assemblies of believers to do the same with their prayers, time, finances, and material resources**   The believers in the first century believed they had all things in common. It was reported that no one lacked among them (Acts 2:44-45; 4:32-34). This sadly is unheard of today.

The common mission of the Kingdom should prompt every ekklesia to be on alert for the needs of other ekklesia in their region (Acts 11:29). The common goal of every ekklesia should be to help foster new ekklesia within their region. This should not be taken lightly. In the Acts 2:42 pattern, prayer was the last activity after continuing in apostolic doctrine, fellowship, and breaking bread. Once this level of '*one voice*' prayer begins, the believers should be seeking directives and strategies from the Holy Spirit to expand beyond themselves. No ekklesia should consider itself to be fully complete until it has helped to give birth to another ekklesia.

Every ekklesia should be self-supporting. Time, finances, material resources, and, I will add, spiritual giftings should be freely given by those in existing gatherings. Effective expansion will result when people who are native to a community, culture, or ethnic group reach their peers with the gospel. Each ekklesia formed should be self-sustaining and capable of reaching others. Therefore, when they give of their time, finances, and material resources, it is not to subsidize new groups. It is the willingness to expend their time, finances, and material resources to reach new believers. This does not negate the responsibility to give to those with legitimate needs, (Acts 11:29; Romans 15:26) but even that type of giving should be to help those in need to become self-sustaining and self-sufficient.

The eight-point definition above gives you a better idea of what the ekklesia is. It will help you during this transition. Gray areas will cause you to second guess your actions and potentially make unnecessary missteps. But this is only the beginning. Remember my friend,

Don Coleman? He challenged us to discover ways to live out ekklesia in our daily faith walk. The next chapter will begin to address that issue.

Wherefore I will not be negligent to put you always in remembrance of these things, though ye know them, and be established in the present truth.

2 Peter 1:12 KJV

## CHAPTER 8:  EKKLESIA TODAY

In chapter 3, I gave you five areas from which we need to transition. First, there must be a transition in how we gather. Second, there must be a transition in how we use resources. Third, we must transition from denominationally based doctrines into the values taught by the first century apostles. Fourth, we must strive to transition from religious and humanistic unity into oneness in Christ. Finally, these are all encased in the overarching reality that we are in the beginning stages of transitioning from a church mindset into what Jesus said He would build — an ekklesia.

As you read this chapter, you should keep in mind what the ekklesia is and what it means to you today. It bears repeating over and over again as it is natural to continue to think 'church'. The ekklesia that Jesus said He would build was historically known by people in the first century as a ruling council. The ekklesia established policies, legislated, conferred or denied citizenship, and elected officials. The ekklesia had ruling powers. Don't let this fact escape you. It is the very basis for Jesus using this word. When He said He would build His ekklesia, He knew those around Him would understand the implications. Jesus surely knew that the ekklesia was a ruling and governing body.

Here we are, two thousand years later, asking, 'how will this look today?' If the twenty-first century ekklesia is a ruling council, then what are its' perimeters? How does the contemporary ekklesia legislate, govern, set policies, and confer or deny citizenship in the twenty-first century? Are there tangible things that we can point to that will differentiate an ekklesia/ruling council from traditional 'church' gatherings? The way believers gather today — auditorium style or house to house — does it make a difference? These questions must be addressed. The fact that there are no strong examples of 21$^{st}$ century ekklesia, makes answering them somewhat problematic. It is imperative that we rely on the Word of God to answer these questions because we often resist what we do not understand.

My wife recently reminded me of the reaction we received when I first taught about the Kingdom in the late 1980's. Many thought we were teaching some fringe or heretical doctrine. It was the same reactions when I taught about deliverance from demons in the early 1990's and the five-fold ministry gifts in the late nineties. None of these teachings were considered popular or mainstream at the time. Today, they are being taught in some of the most conservative denominations, as well as by some of our local critics.

Transitioning from church to ekklesia may evoke similar responses. Whereas some around the country are beginning to teach this, the great majority of believers have no clue that a difference exists. Add to this fact that some who know the history of ekklesia, refuse to consider it relevant to us today. Others may conclude that our interpretation of historical events regarding the mistranslation is wrong. But I must go on record as saying that I believe the Holy Spirit is drawing attention to the difference between church and ekklesia in this season. Whether people accept or deny it cannot be the determining factor for releasing this revelation.

So, let's get back to discussing the tangible differences between a church and an ekklesia. The remainder of this chapter will address the six questions I posed earlier.

## I. How will this (the ekklesia) look today?

And they, <u>continuing daily with one accord in the temple, and breaking bread from house to house</u>, did eat their meat with gladness and singleness of heart, (Acts 2:46)

And <u>daily in the temple, and in every house</u>, they ceased not to teach and preach Jesus Christ. (Acts 5:42)

And Saul was consenting unto his death. And at that time there was a great persecution against the [ruling council] which was at Jerusalem; <u>and they were all scattered abroad throughout the regions of Judaea and Samaria, except the apostles.</u> (Acts 8:1)

131

The Day of Pentecost, as recorded in Acts 2, set in motion one of the greatest transitions in history. Three thousand were baptized that day, and their religious roots immediately collided with the apostles' doctrine. God had moved — literally. With the entrance of the Holy Spirit, God left the man-made temple, and took up residence in man. The rituals of the temple were the only reference points these new believers had for approaching God. Therefore, in the immediate aftermath of the phenomenon on The Day of Pentecost, they tried to reconcile what they knew with what they were learning. They gathered daily in the temple and with other believers in homes. Proponents of the traditional church suggest that the mere mention of the temple justifies meeting in dedicated buildings today. However, history does not support this assertion.

Between eighteen to twenty-four months after the Day of Pentecost, another major issue took place. Stephen was stoned, and severe persecution arose against the believers in Jerusalem. As a result, the new believers fled Jerusalem, leaving only the apostles behind. From that point, there was no more mention of the believers gathering in the temple. Every reference to believers gathering thereafter showed that they met in homes. Understanding this will help paint a clearer picture of how the transition from church to ekklesia will look over the coming years.

> The [ruling councils] of Asia salute you. Aquila and Priscilla salute you much in the Lord, with the [ruling council] that is in their house. (1 Corinthians 16:19)

Salute the brethren which are in Laodicea, and Nymphas, and the [ruling council] which is in his house. (Colossians 4:15)

And to our beloved Apphia, and Archippus our fellowsoldier, and to the [ruling council] in thy house: (Philemon 1:2)

As the understanding of ekklesia grows among believers, there will be attempts to reconcile it with the church as we know and understand it. In my research, I have listened to messages that spoke in glowing terms about the ekklesia, but kept it encased in church rhetoric. There are books written with Ekklesia in the title, but whose contents only included aspects of the church. I recently attended a service where the pastor invited all in attendance to an evening gathering where they would 'do ekklesia'. He spoke as though ekklesia was a program or event being sponsored by their church.

I have had the opportunity to discuss this topic with various leaders. Each of them were genuinely intrigued by what I shared with them. One evangelist shared with me his vision of the 'church'. Interestingly, he described the church by the attributes of the ekklesia. His description helped me to see how deeply ekklesia and church have become synonymous in our beliefs. Without the Holy Spirit, it will be difficult for many to separate themselves from 'church' to embrace ekklesia (John 14:26; 16:13). It may be that, like the persecution that drove the believers out of Jerusalem in the first century, spiritual and cultural factors may come that will draw a line of demarcation between the church and the ekklesia.

Her priests have violated my law, and have profaned mine holy things: <u>they have put no difference between the holy and profane, neither have they shewed difference between the unclean and the clean</u>, and have hid their eyes from my sabbaths, and I am profaned among them. (Ezekiel 22:26)

Then they that feared the LORD spake often one to another: and the LORD hearkened, and heard it, and a book of remembrance was written before him for them that feared the LORD, and that thought upon his name. And they shall be mine, saith the LORD of hosts, in that day when I make up my jewels; and I will spare them, as a man spareth his own son that serveth him. <u>Then shall ye return, and discern between the righteous and the wicked, between him that serveth God and him that serveth him not.</u> (Malachi 3:16-18)

Over the centuries, the institutional church has accumulated a lot of baggage. Rather than changing culture to reflect Kingdom values, it has assimilated itself into society to the point that it has little or no voice on major issues. Today, as we look at the church world, we see an entity that is divided by doctrine, race, and ideology. There is constant infighting over doctrinal issues. Most 'churches' are primarily of one race and ethnic group. In recent years, the 'church' is exhibiting more and more confusion over what is, or is not, sin. The ekklesia cannot be divided like the church because it is *the [ruling council] of the living God, the pillar and ground of the truth.* (1 Timothy 3:15)

Ezekiel prophesied against the priest who mingled the holy with the profane and the clean with the unclean. I believe the emergence of ekklesia is the dawning of a 'Malachi Moment'. Malachi prophesied of a time when there will be a discerning between what is righteous, and what is wicked. In that season, it will be clear who serves God and who does not. The ekklesia will be recognized by the righteous standard they uphold at all cost.

Some ekklesia will be openly contending with the dark forces of government, education, media, arts, entertainment, family, and even religion. Others will be dismantling demonic strongholds in accurate, targeted prayer and intercession. But they all will serve the Lord Jesus Christ as one body. The carnal things that divide the church will not exist among them.

How will the ekklesia look today? I see literally millions of believers, brought together by the Holy Spirit into thousands of small groups to address specific areas in their families, communities, cities, states, and beyond. They won't be contained in dedicated buildings. They will be free to address whatever the Lord has assigned to them. At the same time, they won't be void of leadership. They will be kept safe by elders and equipped for the work they do by the five-fold ministry gifts.

2.  **If the Lord's ekklesia is a ruling council, what are they governing?**
    In both the old and new testaments, the ekklesia governed the affairs of a city or region. Today, cities, counties, states, and even the nations are governed by elected officials. The ekklesia that the Lord is building does not represent local governments, nor are they elected. The Lord's ekklesia is made up of believers who are called out by Him to represent the Kingdom of God in the earth. The first declaration that Jesus made about His ekklesia had to do with its capacity and legislative authority. First, the Gates of

Hades would not be able to overcome it. Therefore, whenever His ekklesia engages in any conflict with the enemy, it will do so knowing that they will ultimately be undefeated (Matthew 16:18; 2Corinthians 2:14; IJohn 5:4-5). This is not to imply that the battles will be simple or painless. It means that any ekklesia He builds will have the divine capacity to defeat the forces of darkness (Romans 8:37; IJohn 4:4).

Second, legislatively, the Lord's ekklesia would be given authority to bind and loose in the earth anything that had already been bound and loosed in the heavens. If it is legal or not legal in the kingdom of heaven, the ekklesia could declare the same as legal or not legal in the earth. The Lord's words clearly mirrored the historical role of the ekklesia.

From the beginning, man was given the mandate to subdue the earth and take back what had been stolen and decimated by satan (Genesis 1:28). Man was placed in a defined territory, the Garden of Eden. Man was given specific instructions to dress and keep it[1] (Genesis 2:15). This two-fold command gives us insight into the Lord's expectation of His ekklesia.

Wherever we are placed by the Holy Spirit, we are to dress and keep that area. Man was never given authority to operate outside of his assigned territory. If he obeyed God, he would be fruitful,

---

[1] 'Dress' is translated from the Hebrew word *'abad*. It's definition implies that man had to work to maintain the garden. The Hebrew word that is translated as 'keep' is *shamar*. This word means to guard. Thus, to dress and keep means that man had to both work to maintain his assignment, and simultaneously protect it from outside attacks.

and the multiplying and replenishing aspect of the command would result in the borders of the garden expanding.

In that assigned place, man's obedience empowered him to subdue anything that opposed the purposes of God. Please understand this point. Man was only given authority to govern the territory that was given to him. The cookie cutter approach to ministry utilized by most churches is a far cry from the strategies given by the Lord.

> To the intent that now unto the principalities and powers in heavenly places might be known by the [ruling council] the manifold wisdom of God, according to the eternal purpose which he purposed in Christ Jesus our Lord: (Ephesians 3:10-11)
>
> For we wrestle not against flesh and blood, but against principalities, against powers, against the rulers of the darkness of this world, against spiritual wickedness in high places. (Ephesians 6:12)

The contemporary ekklesia must realize that its primary battle is in the spirit realm. What is seen in the natural realm should reflect what has taken place in the heavens. That is why each ekklesia must know their assignment, their territory, and be diligent to maintain and guard it.

3. **How does the Lord's ekklesia legislate, govern, set policies, and confer or deny citizenship in the twenty-first century?**

Jesus first declared that an ekklesia built on the revelation of who He is, would be able to overcome the Gates of Hades. He then said that He would give them the keys of the Kingdom of Heaven. With these keys, the ekklesia would be able to bind and loose on earth, those things that are bound and loosed in heaven. In the Charles B. Williams Translation,[1] Matthew 16:19 reads as follows:

> and whatever you forbid on earth must be what is already forbidden in heaven, and whatever you permit on earth must be what is already permitted in heaven

The New American Standard Bible[2] says:

> and whatever you shall bind on earth shall have been bound in heaven and whatever you shall loose on earth shall have been loosed in heaven

The Amplified Bible[3] says:

> and whatever you bind (declare to be improper and unlawful) on earth must be what is already bound in heaven: and whatever you loose (declare lawful) on earth must be what is already loosed in heaven

When the disciples asked Jesus to teach them how to pray, He instructed them to declare, "Thy kingdom come, thy will be done, on earth *as it is* in heaven" (Matthew 6:10). In other words, these all point to the fact that whatever we do on earth, must be already determined in heaven. Jesus, our perfect example, said that He only did what He saw the Father do (John 5:19). The

---

[1] *The New Testament: A Translation in the Language of the People* by Charles B. Williams. © 1937 by Bruce Humphries, Inc. Copyright © renewed 1965 by Edith S. Williams. MOODY BIBLE INSTITUTE

[2] *The New American Standard Bible, New Testament* © 1960, 1962, 1963 by The Lockman Foundation

[3] *The Amplified Bible, Expanded Edition* © 1987 by the Zondervan Corporation and the Lockman Foundation

contemporary ekklesia has been given full authority to legislate. That is, if God has determined something to be illegal in heaven, the ekklesia can declare it illegal on earth.

## GUARDING AND MAINTAINING

Several years ago, we believed God wanted us to address a local street where drugs were rampant. The strategy we had was simple. We took a team down to that street and positioned ourselves near one of the known drug houses. As people drove by, or went in or came out of the drug house, we offered them a bible and prayed for those who would allow us. We did this for several hours and left. A few months later, the drug house was raided by the police and to this day it has not operated again. We did this as 'church folks' with a desire to please the Lord and win souls.

Looking back, it was clear that heaven had declared the activities on that street illegal from a spiritual perspective. We came into agreement with heaven, confronted that gate of Hades, and saw results. If we had understood the revelation of ekklesia at that time, after the drug house was shut down by the raid, we would have sought the Lord as to how we could maintain, guard, and make that area bear fruit for the Kingdom of God.

Let's briefly discuss the governing aspect of the ekklesia in modern times. The contemporary ekklesia must be diligent to govern itself. In the 1920's, mission groups began to realize that in planting 'churches' they should be training indigenous leaders. Roland Allen in his book, *THE SPONTANEOUS EXPANSION OF*

*THE CHURCH: AND THE CAUSES THAT HINDER IT,* discussed how some missionaries taught that native 'churches' should be *self-propagating, self-supporting, and self-governing*[1].

> If the Churches of our foundation are to be self-extending in the sense of self-propagating, they must necessarily possess the power to create their like, and unless they are self-governing and self-supporting they cannot possibly propagate themselves.

This quote from nearly ninety years ago can easily apply to the contemporary ekklesia. It too must have the power to create more ekklesia that are self-supporting and self-governing. This promotes both strength and perpetuity.

Closely linked to being self-governing, the contemporary ekklesia can establish policies. I believe the policies that are established are for the efficient operation of local ekklesia. This is the responsibility of elders. They must provide a safe atmosphere for the local ekklesia to operate. The scope of this book cannot cover every detail of the elders' work, but the following will give you a summary.

Elders must be qualified (I Timothy 3:1-7; Titus 1:5-9; I Peter 5:1-3). An elder must be made an overseer by the Holy Spirit (Acts 20:28; I Peter 5:1-2). His house must be in order (I Timothy 3:4-5). He must have the capacity to feed the flock of God, and protect it against attacks (Acts 20:28-31). An elder

---

[1] *The Spontaneous Expansion of the Church: and the Causes Which Hinder It* by Roland Allen. First Published 1927 Public Domain

must teach sound doctrine (Titus 1:9-11). He must be mature and able to serve without partiality (I Timothy 3:6).

Throughout scripture, it is evident that the elders served in teams. The Old and New Testament confirm the fact that a plurality of elders is God's form of government. In the Old Testament, elders governed the nation (Exodus 24:1; Numbers 22:7). In the New Testament, they governed cities and ekklesia (Acts 14:23; Titus 1:5). Elders did not, or do not govern alone. There was always a plurality of elders. The purpose of this plurality is to provide safety and accountability. The elders, as a team can establish policies that assist ruling councils to fulfill their assignments from the Lord.

Following the authority to establish policy, the ekklesia can also confer or deny citizenship. The institutional church looks for *members* to support their organization. The ekklesia recognizes that God only uses citizens of His Kingdom to do His work. Each citizen must have a revelation of Jesus as the Christ, son of the living God. These Kingdom citizens are believers who have been equipped for the work of ministry. Elders are charged with insuring that no wolf infiltrates the Kingdom citizenry, and the ranks of the ruling councils. There should always be a heart to reconcile anyone who is disruptive to the work. But there must also be a resolve to dismiss anyone who rejects reconciliation or restoration (Matthew 18:15-17; ICorinthians 5:1-5; Galatians 6:1).

4.  Are there tangible things that we can point to that will differentiate an ekklesia/ruling council from other traditional gatherings?

The ability to see the difference between what we know as 'church' and ekklesia will take some time. It is important that you begin to see the differences in practical terms. Everything we have done in 'church' takes on an entirely different dimension in the ekklesia. If you identify with ekklesia, you must be able to identify with it on every level.

The following chart contrasts key areas for you to consider. This by no means is an exhaustive list, but it will help you to begin seeing the differences that exist.

|  | CHURCH | EKKLESIA |
| --- | --- | --- |
| Jesus Christ | Spoken of as Lord, but is often portrayed in light of the church doctrinal distinction | The Christ, Son of the Living God. Lord over the ekklesia and everyone in it |
| Scripture | Used to support denominational and doctrinal distinction | Used to gain divine wisdom and strategies for Kingdom advancement and warfare |
| Evangelism | Winning souls with an unspoken, underlying focus to fill the pews for greater membership | Sole focus is to expand the Kingdom of God through making disciples of nations, and individuals |
| Prayer | Personal needs of the individual and the needs of the church | Seek strategies for taking and occupying territory |

142

| | | |
|---|---|---|
| **Doctrine** | Concerned with being doctrinally correct and distinct from others | Unifying directives based on values, that strengthen and help build the Body of Christ |
| **Word of God** | Comfortable with being only hearers of the Word | Committed to become doers of the Word |
| **Ministry Gifts** | Trained to function and serve within the denominational and local church system. Relies heavily on the gift | Trained and released to impact specific territory. Relies heavily on the Holy Spirit and character of the believer |
| **Leadership** | Hierarchal positions who control the affairs of the church | Servants who serve from the bottom up, for the purpose of strengthening the work of ministry |
| **Gathering** | Believers contained in dedicated building | Believers gathering and becoming a ruling council with binding and loosing authority in specific areas |
| **The Body of Christ** | Divided by sectarian beliefs, race and ideology | Divided by geography, but one in heart and mind |
| **Building** | The Old Testament mindset where God dwells in the building. Lip service is given to the idea that Christ is in us, but buildings are still treated as sacred places | Christ in us. Our body is the Temple of the Holy Spirit. Christ dwells in buildings not made by human hands |

143

| | | |
|---|---|---|
| Membership | A commitment to a specific church group and/or denomination, with adherence to its beliefs and policies | Citizens of the Kingdom of God |
| Giving | Resources collected and used to maintain the 'church' programs, events and operations | Resources used to expand the Kingdom |
| Purpose & Mission | Designed to keep people connected to the church system. Competitive plans and rallying points to build the 'church' | To expand the Kingdom of God in the earth according to the Lord's command in Genesis 1:28 and Matthew 28:19 |

This chart helps to show some of the tangible differences between the church and ekklesia. It helps you to see how either the church or the ekklesia view critical areas. How you see a matter will impact much of what you do. Jesus stated intention is to build an ekklesia, a ruling council with the authority to bind and loose. That is what the believers in the first century saw and understood. The unfortunate switch to the church concept changed His intent and created an insular entity that has redefined the Lord's words.

5. **Does the way believers gather today – auditorium style or house to house – make a difference?**

When I first started writing about 'house church', I received a letter from a man who took issue with one of my blog posts. This is a portion of what he wrote to me:

Is it bad if we are different than the early church? We can easily recognize that the early church did not do it all perfectly either and some things seemingly were not meant to be copied - e.g. pooling all our money as a church. It seems to me that the church learned various things as they went along and maybe, just maybe, it would not be progress to return to some of their early practices. It might indeed be better to research the reasons why they made those changes so that we do not end up re-inventing the wheel, so to speak.

I also wonder about how a move to house churches would affect the world mission effort. *Christianity Today* ran an article a few years ago that showed how by far the bulk of world missions and relief efforts were accomplished by larger churches and denominations. It would be difficult for individual house churches to combine their efforts on a world scale, I am thinking.

This pastor of a conservative denomination believes the current form of gathering has *advanced* the 'church'. He questioned whether it is progress to return to some of the practices of the early 'church'. He suggests that world missions are more effective by larger 'churches' and denominations. In my opinion, the pivotal comment in his letter was, "*It might indeed be better to research the reasons why they made those changes so that we do not end up re-inventing the wheel, so to speak.*" In response, I assert that the changes were not inspired by the Holy Spirit, but rather they came because of satan's attempt to destroy the ekklesia — his greatest threat in the earth.

The first three hundred years after the Day of Pentecost was clearly a time of adjustment and growth. Keep in mind, that what was growing and adjusting was believers — not churches. Believers were learning how to be the ekklesia Jesus said He would build. Without question, there were missteps and failures, and adjustments had to be made. One thing is clear, they did not form denominations, and there were no megachurches. It was millions of believers who gathered (generally from house to house) and who continued to grow under great persecution. Then in about 312 A.D., a dramatic shift took place. Simply put, Christianity went from being persecuted to becoming the state religion.

Believers shifted from the simplicity of gathering from house to house, to meeting in ornate cathedrals. Christianity itself left the love of Christ and became a religious political force. Rather than making disciples, it conducted brutal crusades. Instead of following the leading of the Holy Spirit, pagan gods and worship forms were infused into the religious landscape. During the middle ages, the ekklesia that Jesus said He would build shifted to become kuriakê [oikia], to cirice, to chirche, and now church. Church has become so engrained in our religious and secular cultures that the mere suggestion that this word is wrong sends shivers down denominational spines.

Think about the reformers. Wycliffe, Hus, Calvin, and of course Luther began challenging the religious status quo (albeit in context of the church). In the sixteenth century, Luther's 95 Thesis set in motion the restoration (not reverting), of biblical truths that had been lost. Salvation by grace through faith, holiness, sanctification, water baptism, laying on of hands, the infilling of the Holy Spirit with the present-day manifestation of His

146

gifts, and the five-fold ministry gifts (i.e. prophets and apostles), all resurfaced in our Christian vocabulary. Once again, I reiterate that these things have all taken place under the 'church' umbrella. It should also be noted that it was in the century following Martin Luther, that King James authorized the switch from ekklesia to church.

In recent years, there has been a noticeable decline in 'church' attendance. Adherents to the institutional church usually lay the blame on those leaving. Some have suggested this is the 'great falling away' or apostasy spoken of in the bible. I would suggest that it is neither. Why? Because many of those leaving the institutional church have not left their relationship with Jesus Christ. They only left a system that they believe has lost its authenticity. House, organic, and simple church groups became a plausible choice for those who recognized the continued need for fellowship with other believers. Let me quickly interject that most of these groups did not spring up because the people in them were dysfunctional. That has been a false label imposed upon them by some in the institutional church system.

I believe the pastor's suggestion that we need to understand why certain changes have taken place, have been answered by events in history. In my opinion, the ekklesia was taken off course in the fourth century, and the erroneous trajectory was reinforced by the willful mistranslation of ekklesia to church. How then can the church evolve to something better, when the concept of 'church' should have never existed?

We can mistakenly believe that because the Lord has allowed 'church' to exist for nearly 1,700 years, that it implicitly means He approves of this switch. No. Jesus said He would build His ekklesia, not a church or church system. That has not changed. From the sixteenth century forward, God has progressively restored lost doctrinal truths and the abandoned ministry gifts. Everything has come to this hour. It is the day of the saints. Doctrine that has been interpreted by denominational preferences, and ministry gifts that have been plugged into nonbiblical hierarchal roles, are being corrected by the Holy Spirit. The releasing of the saints will require the restoration of the structure that existed when Jesus declared, "Upon this rock I will build my ekklesia!"

How we gather is multifaceted. Traditional large gatherings play a part in ekklesia and gathering from house to house is also important to the overall operational structure. Both are needed. I also believe there is a third component, that I will discuss in detail in the next chapter. Before you turn the page, remind yourself once again that Jesus said He would build an ekklesia — a ruling council, not a church.

... those who are seriously determined to be Christians and confess the gospel with hand and mouth, must enroll themselves by name and meet apart in one house, for prayer, for reading, to baptize, to take the Sacrament, and exercise other Christian works

Martin Luther

# CHAPTER 9: REVISITING OUR GATHERINGS

My original intent for writing this book was to provide the reader with a roadmap to transition from the 'institutional church' into a network of regional house 'churches'. I was internally conflicted, because such a transition seemed to be no more than changing from one form to another. My notes were strong on 'what' to do, but I felt rather weak in explaining 'why' we were doing it. When I understood what Jesus said at Caesarea Philippi, a light came on in my spirit. Everything I had learned about salvation and redemption, grace and deliverance from demonic bondage, the Kingdom of God, and even ministry gifts made sense in the context of the ekklesia Jesus said He would build.

I am still a strong proponent of gathering from house to house. However, gathering in a living room is not the total picture, or the only way we should interact. The way we gather is not a doctrinal issue. There is no scripture that specifically says, "Thou shalt gather in houses". Yet, the New Testament is filled with ample evidence that the first century believers primarily met in homes rather than dedicated buildings. In this chapter, I will share 'why' I believe we should gather from house to house. I will also show why large gatherings have their place, too. I will reinforce some of what you have already read in previous chapters, and if you have read my book, *NO LONGER CHURCH AS USUAL*, you may recognize similar themes and patterns.

> ## The way we gather is not a doctrinal issue

Over the last few years, I have been leading and teaching the fellowship I serve to gather from house to house, rather than in the building we have used for nearly twenty-five years. This has been a slow but genuinely rewarding process. I am watching the believers embrace this New Testament model, and we are beginning to see the fruit of our labors. In this journey, we have had some great successes, and some heart-breaking failures. My friend, Donald Todd helped me put this in perspective. He shared that we should not look at these successes and failures as win-loss times, instead we should view them as win-learn moments. We rejoice when we get it right, and learn from our missteps and disappointments. All in all, it is, and has been exciting and spiritually rewarding.

## WE ARE MOVING FORWARD

To the outsider looking in, it may look like we are back peddling, as we only gather in our building on the first, third and fifth Sundays. On the second and fourth weeks of the month, the saints have the opportunity and freedom to gather in their homes. Our training is done publicly, and from house to house (Acts 20:20). Believe me when I say that the foundation for impact and effect is being laid. Everyone involved is maturing and growing in covenant relationships with each other.

I believe 'how' we gather is important. If there is one word that can bring clarity to the purpose for any gathering, it would be '*relationship*'. There are five values that form the foundation of doctrine, the fourth of these values is that *we grow through covenant relationships*. If we fail to cultivate strong Godly relationships, our efforts will always be minimized. If we fail to recognize the value in the various kinds of relationships we are involved in, we will impair our ability to be effective. If we misinterpret our role in a relationship, the potential for dysfunction and inappropriateness will be present.

Relationships are critical to ekklesia. They are formed from called out believers who have a revelation of Jesus as the Christ, Son of the Living God. Our fellowship with each other is first contingent upon our relationship with Christ (1John 1:7). If our gatherings are to become effective ruling councils, it is imperative that they are filled

151

with strong mature relationships. Any division and dissention within the ekklesia would be a recipe for disaster and defeat (Mark 3:24; Luke 11:17).

Relationships must be nurtured. Family, home, school and work are the most common places for building strong relationships. The scope of this book will not, and cannot cover the myriad of relationships that exist. We will focus our attention on the relationships that are nurtured among believers in covenant communities. We will highlight the results of healthy relationships in the Body of Christ, and ultimately in the ekklesia.

> And they continued stedfastly in the apostles' doctrine and fellowship, and in breaking of bread, and in prayers. (Acts 2:42)

In Chapter 6, I outlined a pattern from Acts 2:42. If you recall, it began with the commitment to embrace apostolic doctrine. Apostolic doctrine was immediately followed by fellowship. Fellowship is the foundation of strong relationships. The word fellowship is translated from the Greek word *koinonia*. It is used nineteen times throughout the New Testament, but is not always translated as fellowship. In other scriptures, the word *koinonia* is translated as *contribution* (Romans 15:26), *communion* (1Corinthians 10:16), *distribution* (2Corinthians 9:13), *communication* and *communicate* (Philemon 1:6; Hebrews 13:16). Each of these words suggests close relational interaction. They give us a glimpse of how first century believers understood fellowship.

In our western religious mindset, the practice of fellowship is often impersonal and superficial. Sitting in a pew behind someone in a 'church service' of mixed denominations, followed by shaking hands with a stranger from another 'church' in the lobby, and possibly sharing some cookies and punch together, is what often constitutes our version of fellowship. Just as we need to learn and pursue ekklesia, we must also revisit what fellowship means, and how it affects our relationships with each other.

True fellowship requires and investment of time. Believers, from various cultures, ethnic groups, and economic statuses must submit to, and commit to the time it takes to learn from each other (Ephesians 5:21). Sporadic and structured meetings in sterile environments do little to foster lasting relationships. Believers must be willing to step outside of their comfort zones to spend time with other believers within their world experiences, and vice versa. We must learn to see each and experience each other as one in Christ. That will take both time and effort.

> There is neither Jew nor Greek, there is neither bond nor free, there is neither male nor female: for ye are all one in Christ Jesus.

Galatians 3:28 is often used in support of a westernized version of equality in Christ. When it is quoted, the distinctions among us are either ignored, or minimized. Don't misunderstand me. We are all equal in Christ. If anyone, regardless of their sex, culture or social status is baptized into Christ, they have in fact, put on Christ (Galatians 3:27). But we cannot ignore our distinctions and still relate to each other honestly. In this passage, Paul affirms that we are all one in Christ Jesus regardless of our culture (Jew or Greek), our economic status (bond or free), or gender (male or female). We are spiritually equal, but often culturally, economically and gender distinct. Understanding this is an important first step in restoring true biblical fellowship today. Unlike gender or race, a person can change their cultural associations and their economic status, but even then, the distinctions remain.

In a perfect Christian world, believers from all walks of life would regularly gather in homes to reinforce apostolic doctrine, to fellowship, break bread and pray. From these gatherings, ruling councils would form to confront specific Gates of Hades. Unfortunately, we live in a complex world of contradictory religious ideas, fear-based cultural biases, and conflicting beliefs regarding gender roles in the Kingdom. Instead of the Body of Christ, we resemble David's mighty men that joined him in the cave of Abdullum (1 Samuel 22:1-2). They became a powerful force to reckon with, but they did not begin that way. This is the current state of the 'church' that must somehow transition into the ekklesia that Jesus declared He would build.

## FELLOWSHIP AND BREAKING BREAD MUST BE INTENTIONAL

On the Day of Pentecost, Luke reported that Jerusalem was filled with 'devout men, out of every nation under heaven' (Acts 2:5). He lists fifteen nations, each with their own language, cultures and customs.[1] After Peter's powerful message, three thousand people from

---

[1] Online Reference https://www.questia.com/library/journal/1P3-217237561/the-list-of-nations-in-acts-2-roman-propaganda-and The list of nations in Acts 2 were apparently those under Roman control. It was assumed that Rome controlled the known world at that time. Luke's writing attempts to show that all nations belonged to Jesus Christ rather than Caesar.

this mixture of nations were baptized. Twice Luke reports that these new believers met daily in the Temple and from house to house (Acts 2:46; 5:42). They were very intentional about gathering.

Intentionality will in some aspects become the litmus test for believers during this transition. Rather than the weekly ritual of *'going to church'* every Sunday, believers must be, I repeat, must be intentional about connecting with, and gathering with other believers regularly and consistently.

What does it mean to be intentional? It means that you make no excuses for not gathering with other believers. It means that you pursue believers to gather with. It means you are willing to walk with other believers as they address their faults, and be willing to submit to them as you address yours. Being intentional means, you become willing to gather with believers outside of your cultural and economic environment. It also means that you are willing to invite believers from other cultural and economic status into your environment. Being intentional means you seek to understand the life experiences of those you gather with. And finally, to be intentional means that you value your oneness in Christ with other believers more than your cultural, economic, social or gender biases[1].

Luke wrote that the believers broke bread from house to house, and ate their meals with 'gladness and singleness of heart' (Acts 2:46). Favor and numerical growth were by-products of their fellowship.

---

[1] Gender biases refer to beliefs regarding the role of men and women in ministry. It does not include unbiblical concepts of an individual's gender preference.

This reveals the powerful effect of their intentional gatherings. Remember, this began with over fifteen nations, and cultures. Intentional fellowship combined with breaking of bread, help to break down walls of misunderstanding and exposes unwarranted cultural prejudices.

Consider the matter concerning the Grecian widows. The enemy would have loved to use this to stir up division among the saints. Three things were clear. First, those neglected were specifically identified by their culture.

---

**Being intentional means, you become willing to gather with believers outside of your cultural and economic environment**

---

Second, the fact that they were widows suggests their low economic situation. And three, it's ironic that the concern centered around these widows being neglected in the daily provision of food. The fellowship, breaking of bread and the overall idea of eating with gladness and singleness of heart could have been tainted by this oversight, whether accidental or on purpose.

I personally believe that how the apostles handled this matter, and the response of the believers, underscores the strength that had been nurtured. Instead of division over cultural neglect, Luke reported that the solution pleased everyone, and the number of disciples grew and multiplied (Acts 6:5-7).

As believers get to know each other, they become stronger together. Their trust of each other is strengthened. They become one. This is a critical necessity. The forces of darkness will use anything

156

to defeat the Lord's ruling councils. Deception and division have been their primary weapons against the 'institutional church'. Fellowship and breaking bread together will foster godly relationships that will reduce the enemy's ability to use those weapons against the ekklesia.

## LARGE GATHERINGS ARE NEEDED

Three times in the New Testament there are references to the 'whole' ekklesia.

> Then pleased it the apostles and elders, with the <u>whole</u> [ekklesia], to send chosen men of their own company to Antioch with Paul and Barnabas; namely, Judas surnamed Barsabas, and Silas, chief men among the brethren: (Acts 15:22)

> Gaius mine host, and of the <u>whole</u> [ekklesia], saluteth you. Erastus the chamberlain of the city saluteth you, and Quartus a brother. (Romans 16:23)

> If therefore the <u>whole</u> [ekklesia] be come together into one place, and all speak with tongues, and there come in those that are unlearned, or unbelievers, will they not say that ye are mad? (1Corinthians 14:23)

To suggest the existence of a whole ekklesia, is to imply that it is made up of smaller parts. I would suggest that the smaller parts are the gatherings of believers that meet in homes. The whole ekklesia is then a gathering of several individual ruling councils in a specific area.

In Acts, it was the whole ekklesia in Jerusalem that settled the issue of circumcision (Acts 15:1-22). It is also interesting to note that the decision was sent by letter to the Gentile believers in Antioch, Syria and Cilicia. Cilicia and Syria were both provinces of Rome, and Antioch was a principle city located roughly halfway between the two.

When Paul, Barnabas, Judas and Silas arrived, they gathered the *multitude* together to deliver the letter that had been written. Is it possible that this *multitude* was a whole ekklesia consisting of Gentile believers? Were there several Gentile ruling councils in that area? Could there have been multiple gatherings in the regions that met in Antioch to receive the letter?

Let's start from the response the Gentiles had to the massage from Jerusalem. The bible says they rejoiced because of the encouraging words (Acts 15:31). For a while, Paul, Barnabas and Silas remained in Antioch teaching and preaching. Then an unfortunate event happened.

> And some days after Paul said unto Barnabas, Let us go again and visit our brethren in every city where we have preached the word of the Lord, and see how they do. (Acts 15:36)

Paul suggested to Barnabas that they visit the brethren in *every city* where they had preached to see how they were doing. This resulted in a disagreement between them over John Mark. It appears that Mark had left Paul and Barnabas in Pamphylia clandestinely and returned to Jerusalem (Acts 13:13). Paul did not want him to accompany them on this new journey, and Barnabas was adamant that he should. Their disagreement escalated and resulted in a sharp and contentious separation (Acts 15:39).

Paul's suggestion to Barnabas *to visit every city*, reveals the possibility of several Gentile gatherings in the region. It is obvious that there was more than one city where believers were gathering. Unfortunately, Paul and Barnabas got into a fray over John Mark. After their disagreement and separation, Barnabas and Mark sailed to Cyprus, and Paul and Silas went through Syria and Cilicia confirming and strengthening the ekklesia (Acts 15:41). These were Gentile ruling councils that had been previously established by Paul and Barnabas, and were most likely represented in the multitude that gathered in Antioch. It could be considered a Gentile version of the whole ekklesia. I shared this insight to accentuate the fact that larger gatherings, both Jew and Gentile, existed in the first century, and offered specific benefits to the believers.

**Strength** Small isolated groups can become discouraged. It can feel lonely when no one else is gathering house to house in your area. Gathering with other groups builds both confidence and strength (Acts 4:32-33).

**Unity** Jesus prayed that we would be 'one' even as He and the Father were 'one' (John 17:21). By coming together with other groups, more walls are broken down as everyone embraces the single mission to expand the Kingdom of God in their region. The larger gathering of multiple ekklesia will help to eliminate cultural, economic and gender barriers. Even more, Jesus declared that by being one, the world would know that He was sent by God.

**Resources** The bible says that the early believers had all things in common, and that no one lacked among them. This was not communism, but rather common-ism. The needs of all were met (Acts 2:45; 4:34). Together, the believers were also able to meet the needs of the poor (Romans 15:26)

**Protection**  The role of elders is to oversee, protect and feed the flock of God (Acts 20:28; IPeter 5:1-3). Those being served are instructed to 'know who labors among them' (IThessalonians 5:12-13; Hebrews 13:17). The large gatherings allow everyone to know those who are approved to serve them; this includes elders and ministry gifts. To reinforce this, local elders should regularly gather all ekklesia they serve.

**Apostolic Doctrine**  When all the ekklesia in a city or region come together, it is an opportune time to teach apostolic doctrine. It was the multitude of Gentile believers that received the news that they were not required to be circumcised. It was the whole ekklesia in Corinth that was instructed in order and decorum when they gathered (ICorinthians 14:23, 33, 40). The large gatherings serve as a backdrop to providing teaching and clarity to the Body of believers.

It is interesting to note that Paul's letters to nearly every city was addressed to the saints, presumably the whole ekklesia in that area. The only variance was to the Philippi where he added the bishops (elders) and deacons to his salutation, and to the Colossians where he saluted both the saints and the faithful brothers, most likely elders. This suggests that Paul understood the importance of sharing information with the whole ekklesia.[1]

---

[1] Romans 1:7; ICorinthians 1:2; 2Corinthians 1:1; Galatians 1:2; Ephesians 1:1; Philippians 1:1 (includes elders and deacons); Colossians 1:2 (includes faithful brothers most likely elders); 1Thessalonians 1:1; 2Thessalonians 1:1

Gatherings of the whole ekklesia may look like traditional 'church' meetings on the surface. However, it is more effective when the purpose is understood.

## BELIEVERS MUST BE TAUGHT

The foundation of all gatherings begins in the house. It is there that the *presence* of Christ is realized. Then, all house gatherings in a city or region should come together for corporate praise, worship, unity and instruction. In these gatherings of the whole ekklesia, the power of Christ is experienced. Finally, there must be specific times of teaching so that the *purpose* of Christ can be understood.

In this season of transition, teaching will be extremely important. Yes, the Holy Spirit is the great teacher, but He often uses men and women to impart spiritual truths to believers. Most of the New Testament letters written by Paul, was in fact, him teaching matters critical and necessary for the Body of Christ. He taught the Kingdom of God in the synagogues, the school of Tyrannus, and from a house he rented (Acts 19:8-10; 28:30).

Teaching is more than simply providing new information; it often helps people to unlearn false information. Everyone reading this book has some knowledge of 'church'. It has been engrained into our spirits and minds all our lives. Now, when we learn that the word 'church' was a mistranslation, and should have never been used, there is immediate resistance and apprehension in our hearts. I know. I too felt the same thing. But facts, are facts. Once you know the facts, you become responsible for how you handle them.

161

I realize I am being somewhat repetitious. But it needs to be said over and over again, that the truth about ekklesia is not new information. God is bringing this revelation to the forefront by apostles and prophets in this season (Ephesians 3:5). Ekklesia was the word Jesus used at Caesarea Philippi to describe what He would build. That has never changed. Although some may argue as to why it was mistranslated, it cannot be disputed that King James prompted the change. We may not agree on the effect this change has had on the Body of Christ, but you cannot ignore the fact that the words 'church' and 'ekklesia' have two different meanings and histories.

Some may not feel a need to implement contemporary versions of ekklesia, but you cannot ignore that what Jesus said He would build, and what we have today, are completely different. This all comes down to teaching. Believers must be taught. The five-fold ministry gifts are charged with equipping the saints for the work of ministry. This boils down to teaching from the various disciplines they have been given (i.e. apostolic, prophetic, evangelistic, etc.). Once you have the information, you become responsible to either validate it or reject it based upon the Word of God.

We do not serve God in a vacuum. We function in a Body, that has been fitly joined together for God's purpose in the earth. Each of us has a part that is important to the whole body. Therefore, we must intentionally gather with other believers. As we gather from house to house, *covenant* relationships among the believers develop. As we come together in gatherings of the whole ekklesia in a city or region, Godly *connections* are established that strengthen us all. And finally, as believers are provided classes for specific teaching, *clarity* of the Word of God and divine purpose is revealed.

Through covenant, connection and clarity, we become poised to experience the transition from church to ekklesia. If you are ready, we can go forward with courage and confidence as we allow Jesus to build us into the ekklesia that will confront the Gates of Hades.

YOU MAY CHOOSE TO LOOK THE OTHER WAY,
BUT YOU CAN NEVER SAY AGAIN THAT YOU DID
NOT KNOW

WILLIAM WILBERFORCE

# CHAPTER 10: WHERE DO WE GO FROM HERE?

My purpose for writing *LEAVING CHURCH BECOMING EKKLESIA* has been three-fold. First, I wanted you to understand how the word church was injected into the Christian world. Second, I wanted you to begin seeing the possibility of the ekklesia functioning in the earth today. Third, I wanted to lay the foundation necessary for you to begin the transition from church to ekklesia.

Whether you embrace my conclusions or not, it is still important that you reconcile the historical facts with the Word of God. Jesus never said He would build a 'church'. When King James replaced *ekklesia* with the word *church*, it changed the trajectory of God's people in the earth. Instead of being a ruling council that would confront the Gates of Hades, it became a docile entity more comfortable with being insular and isolated. Church became identified as the building to which we go to, or a religious sect to which we belong. If ekklesia had remained, today we would be identified as a called-out body of believers who represent the Kingdom of God.

Identifying with ekklesia without pursuing its purpose for existence is pointless. Jesus knew exactly what He would build; a powerful ruling council, not a church. I believe He is still building His ekklesia today. You and I are the lively stones being built into a spiritual house. We are being built together as a holy habitation of God through the Spirit (Ephesians 2:21-22; 1Peter 2:5). I want you to grasp the reality that contemporary ruling councils can exist. Under Jesus Christ, they can make indelible marks in culture that expand the Kingdom of God.

How do we begin to lay the foundation necessary to begin the transition from church to ekklesia? I have touched on this in previous chapters, and will conclude this book with more instruction that I pray will motivate you to pursue this transition. This final chapter is both a summary and a call to action.

## THE PRESENT TRUTH

Let's begin by making sure you understand the purpose of God in this season. You must begin by "...*being established in the present truth*". (2Peter 1:12)

> And He gave some as apostles, and some as prophets, and some as evangelists, and some as pastors and teachers, ***for the equipping of the saints***

*for the work of service,* to the building up of the body of Christ; (Ephesians 4:11-12 NASB)

This is the day of the saints. Beginning with the reformation in the sixteenth century, several key things have been restored to the Body of Christ. Basic doctrines such as salvation by grace through faith, sanctification, holiness, and water baptism have been restored. The gifts of the Holy Spirit, including healing, prophecy, and speaking in tongues have been restored.

> This is the day of the saints. If you are a believer, this is your day. God desires to empower and release you.

And, the ministry gifts of the apostles, prophets, evangelist, pastors, and teachers have been restored.

These were not restored to be hijacked by religious systems or encased by denominational boundaries. They were restored to reinstate God's original intent to fill the earth with men and women who live out the Kingdom Mandate (Genesis 1:28). They were restored so that the saints can be equipped for the work of ministry (Ephesians 4:12). They were restored to release an army of believers who will go into the world to make disciples of all nations (Matthew 28:19).

This is the day of the saints. If you are a believer, this is your day. God desires to empower and release you. You are living in the day of the saints. God knew you would be born and available in this season (Acts 17:26). His desire is to activate and use you to expand His Kingdom rule in the earth. Understanding this should stir you to do what it takes to be *"...a vessel for honor, sanctified, and suitable for the master's use, prepared for every good work"* (2Timothy 2:21). This is the present truth that must be taught with urgency.

## FRESH RELEASE OF APOSTOLIC DOCTRINE

Like Paul, this is the third time I will approach this topic of apostolic doctrine in this book (2Corinthians 13:1). In Acts 2:42, Luke stated that the believers followed apostolic doctrine before anything else. In this time of transition, apostolic doctrine will be a necessity to help believers navigate the transition from church to ekklesia.

What is apostolic doctrine, and how does it look today? It always begins with the foundation of Jesus Christ. Jesus declared that He would build His ekklesia with those who have a revelation of Him as the Christ, Son of the Living God. Contemporary apostles must insure that every believer they serve is thoroughly taught the Jesus of scripture (1Corinthians 15:3-8). It then becomes the work of the Holy Spirit to reveal Jesus as Lord to each person (1Corinthians 12:3).

Apostolic doctrine brings clarity to events and articulates divine purpose. Remember Peter clarified the events that took place on the Day of Pentecost. He tied the phenomenon the crowd was witnessing to the prophetic writings of Joel. He shared God's intent to pour out of His Spirit on all flesh (Joel 2:28). After his conversion, Paul revealed God's will to bring the Gentiles into the Kingdom (Romans 15:16; Ephesians 3:6). He referred to Old Testament writings to show this was God's eternal intent (Genesis 18:18; Galatians 3:8).

Just as it was in the first century, the vast majority of people had no clue what was happening on the Day of Pentecost (Acts 2:12-13). Only a mere 120 people had experienced the infilling of the Holy Spirit. Peter had to explain this to a crowd that had several hundred years of religious ritual and presuppositions. Most Jews did not understand, or even rejected, the fact that salvation was available to the Gentiles (Acts 13:46-48). Paul preached the revelation God gave him against an historical wall of Judaic dominance. Even Peter struggled for a time with that revelation. It took the Holy Spirit to reveal it to Him, then to some of the other Jews and, of course, to the Gentiles (Acts 10:34, 45-46; 11:17-18).

> Being *one* does not mean we will always agree on *what* we do, but we must all agree on *why* we are doing it.

> And it shall come to pass afterward, **that I will pour out my spirit upon all flesh; and your sons and your daughters shall prophesy, your old men shall dream dreams, your young men shall see visions: And also upon the servants and upon the handmaids in those days will I pour out my spirit**. And I will shew wonders in the heavens and in the earth, blood, and fire, and pillars of smoke. The sun shall be turned into darkness, and the moon into blood, before the great and the terrible day of the LORD come. And it shall come to pass, **that whosoever shall call on the name of the LORD shall be delivered:** for in mount Zion and in Jerusalem shall be deliverance, as the LORD hath said, and in the remnant whom the LORD shall call. (Joel 2:28-32)

The idea that the gift of the Holy Spirit, and all the accompanying manifestations, would be available to all was not new. It had always been in the mind of God. It was always in the heart of our Father to have a Kingdom of Priest (Exodus 19:6; 1Peter 2:9). The fact that salvation would be available to the Gentiles was not new. That too, was always in the heart of God (Isaiah 42:6; 49:6; 60:1-3).

Likewise, ekklesia is not new. The first occurrence of the ekklesia is found in the Old Testament. The Hebrew word qahal was translated in the Septuagint[1] as ekklesia (Deuteronomy 9:10; 18:16). It clearly referred to a people called out for God's purposes.

Jesus said He would build His ekklesia – not church. That cannot be disputed. It cannot be overstated. The response to this truth will undoubtedly invoke a wide range of reactions.

> And God blessed them, and God said unto them, Be fruitful, and multiply, and replenish the earth, and subdue it: and have dominion over the fish of the sea, and over the fowl of the air, and over every living thing that moveth upon the earth. (Genesis 1:28)

> Go ye therefore, and teach all nations, baptizing them in the name of the Father, and of the Son, and of the Holy Ghost: (Matthew 28:19)

Apostolic Doctrine must embrace the Kingdom Mandate. From the beginning, God intended for man to be His vice-regents in the earth. Jesus reiterated that command with the expectation that we would go into all the world making disciples. The authority of the ekklesia is found in the language of both the Kingdom Mandate and the Great Commission.

The Kingdom Mandate commands us to be fruitful and to multiply and fill the earth. It culminates with the command to subdue

---

[1] The Septuagint is a translation of the Hebrew Bible and some related texts into Koine Greek.

and have dominion. Subduing would be unnecessary if the potential for conflict didn't exist. Dominion implies there are other authorities seeking to rise above the purposes of God.

The Great Commission begins with Jesus declaring that all authority in both heaven and earth had been given to Him. It was then that He told His disciples to "Go!" Why would He proclaim His authority before releasing them? Mark and John clarify this for us.

The same works that Jesus did during His earthly ministry, would be done by believers (Mark 16:16-18; John 14:12). Even when Jesus declared He would build His ekklesia, He promised to give the keys of the Kingdom of Heaven to His followers and made it clear that Hades gates would not prevail against them.

The Kingdom Mandate and the Great Commission give the ekklesia a purpose for existing. They each express the intent of the Father. He expects every ruling council to be fruitful, to multiply and replenish the earth, and to subdue it and have dominion in it. The marching orders, for all ekklesia, is to go into all the world making disciples of all nations.


## ALL EKKLESIA MUST FUNCTION AS ONE

Division and dissention have no place in the Lord's ekklesia. Whether they are in West Quoddy Head, Maine or Cape Wrangell, Alaska, every ekklesia must stand on the same firm foundation. As ruling councils are called out around the country, each person must accept the doctrine of Christ as the only doctrine (Hebrew 6:1-2). They must be willing to submit to apostolic doctrine for vision, clarity, and continuity (Acts 2:42). And, any doctrine they personally embrace must not violate the Word of God, the Doctrine of Christ, or apostolic doctrine (1Corinthians 14:26).

Jesus prayed that we would be 'one' (John 17:11). Paul exhorted the Corinthians to be of 'one heart and one mind' (1Corinthians 1:10). Our oneness will be crucial in the coming days. The enemy will pounce on any place of division and discontent. Being *one* does not mean we will always agree on *what* we do, but we must all agree on *why* we are doing it.

The ekklesia and everyone serving in it are ambassadors of the Kingdom of Heaven. Their mission is to expand the rule of the Kingdom throughout the earth. Some may be assigned to government, while another ekklesia may be confronting demonic influence in the media. One ruling council may bring kingdom principles into local business, while others challenge the enemy's attempt to distort the family structure. They all are led by the Lord Jesus Christ, and know how to uproot strongholds with strategic prayer. The final goal is that the kingdoms of this world will become the Kingdom of our God and of His Christ (1Corinthians 15:24; Revelation 11:15).

It is critical that we approach our individual assignments embracing the same values. Values that are understood and embraced help us to understand each other's motives and increase our ability to walk together as one. Values precede doctrine. They are usually unwritten, but understood and practiced with no conscious forethought. Every family, community, culture, and religion has foundational values that drive how life is lived among them. Day to day decisions are based on the values they embrace.

Too often, core values have been lost. What begins with a clear purpose gets diluted into religious rhetoric. To clarify the values of the first century ekklesia, the apostles (most notably

> Doctrines become divisive when the core values they were to clarify are lost

Paul), wrote many letters to the fledgling ruling councils. He established doctrine to help them navigate within the new Kingdom culture Jesus had introduced (Acts 2:42; I Corinthians 4:17). Unfortunately, people often camp around pet doctrines – debating their merits, while missing the core values that necessitated them. Today institutional churches have established doctrinal statements, but have often missed the core values that drive their beliefs.

Doctrines become divisive when the core values they were to clarify are lost. I baptize this way – you baptize that way; I speak in tongues – you don't speak in tongues; I believe this – you believe that; and we remain in our little camps convincing ourselves that our doctrines are the right ones. Literally thousands of denominations have emerged whose sole existence is based upon the doctrines they choose to camp around. The devil has used our idolization of pet doctrines to keep the institutional church divided and weak (Mark 3:24; I Timothy 4:1). I believe doctrine is important. I also believe that the purpose for any doctrine is to help clarify the values of the Kingdom of God.

In my book, *NO LONGER CHURCH AS USUAL*, I detail five primary values that I believe serve as the foundation for most doctrine.[1] They are, (1) The Lordship of Jesus Christ, (2) The Priesthood of every believers, (3) The present-day manifestation of the Holy Spirit gifts, (4) Growing, spiritually and numerically through covenant relationships, and (5) that no one among us shall lack. The challenge going forward is, for believers who understand ekklesia, to allow the Holy Spirit to strip away divisive beliefs that keep us weak and ineffective. This by no means intended to eliminate doctrine. Sound doctrine is important (Titus 2:1). But anytime our doctrine causes division, confusion, or dissention, we must allow the Holy Spirit to address this. This is for the good of the Kingdom of God. We begin this process by sitting and praying with our brothers and sisters at the feet of Jesus, in one heart, soul and mind (Matthew 22:36-40; Acts 2:1; 4:31-32).

## THE RULING COUNCIL IN YOUR NEIGHBORHOOD

If you are beginning to grasp the reality of the ekklesia, you may be wondering where to find such a ruling council in your community? The answer may surprise you. It begins with you.

You should spend time praying and fasting over this matter. You should search this out in the word of God.[2] You should confirm the

---

[1] NO LONGER CHURCH AS USUAL *Second Edition* Pages 162 - 183

[2] See Chapters 4 and 6 of this book. How Ekklesia Became Church and Activating Ekklesia

history of the words church and ekklesia.[1] Then, follow the leading of the Holy Spirit. Share this with those He tells you to, and allow Him to connect you with others who are also beginning to understand this truth. You may suggest that they read this book. As He connects you with other believers, establish times to meet with them to pray and seek the Lord in this matter. Use Appendix A at the end of this book to guide your gatherings.

Gathering with other believers does not mean that you are automatically a full-fledged, functioning ekklesia. You must wait on the Lord to call you out for a specific purpose. Remember, the apostles were first told to wait in Jerusalem until they received power from on high (Luke 24:48-49). No, this is not an attempt to recreate the Day of Pentecost, but rather a reminder for you to understand the principle of waiting on the Lord for instructions (Isaiah 40:31).

As you wait, you can research and study apostolic doctrine together. While you wait, you can fellowship and break bread together (Acts 2:42). You should gather regularly and consistently; especially in the early days. Allow the Holy Spirit to strengthen the covenant among you.

Do not become isolated. Although ekklesia is not new, the implementation of it is. Trying to connect with other gatherings may be a challenge. I will keep you updated regularly through my blog[2] or on

---

[1] See Suggested Resources

[2] www.ekklesiacenter.org/blog

my Facebook page. Join Ekklesia United[1]; a new online forum that is being developed to give those around the country an opportunity to network. Make local connections where you can, and trust God for growth in your area.

I would like to interject a strong word of caution. At times when small groups meet, the discussion turns toward criticism of former 'churches' or church leaders. You should avoid such conversations at all cost. What Jesus is building with you is based on your *revelation* of Him, not the perceived flaws you see in others. It is a waste of time, and dishonoring to God to use times of fellowship as a platform to criticize others. God has graciously allowed you to see the difference between church and ekklesia, and that knowledge does not give you the right to attack those who do not understand it yet. What you have learned does not elevate you above other believers. It only means that God has trusted you to accurately handle revealed truth. I challenge you to be a good steward over this and any other revelation you receive.

> What Jesus is building with you is based on your *revelation* of Him, not the perceived flaws you see in others

Each time you gather you should pray and partake of the Lord's Table (I Corinthians 11:26). It is not necessary to have an 'ordained

---

[1] www.ekklesiaunited.org

clergy' present to do this. Nowhere in scripture is that a requirement. Trust God. The Lord's Table is an ordinance for all believers·

Of course, anytime you gather you should pray together. The focus of your prayers may change over time. First, you should pray with, and for, each other. Pray for any needs among those in the gathering. Be willing to serve each other in resolving needs and concerns. Second, pray for other groups that may be gathering in your city and around the country. Third, pray with us, as we trust God to reveal the truth about ekklesia to believers across this nation. Fourth, pray for those who don't know Jesus Christ in your neighborhood, your city, and your region. This is all futile if the net result doesn't bring people into the saving knowledge of our Lord. The Kingdom expands as people are drawn out of darkness into the Kingdom of Jesus Christ (Colossians 1:13).

Finally, pray for your assignment. What does the Lord want you to do? An ekklesia has a mission. No two ruling councils may be alike, but they are all fulfilling a purpose of the King. Once you know what you are called out to do, seek the Lord for strategy and implementation. God is creative. Don't limit Him. Go forth with confidence, knowing that you are more than conquerors through Christ Jesus (Romans 8:37; 2Corinthians 2:14).

## DECISION TIME

Some will read this book and simply set it aside as irrelevant. Others will consider this talk about ekklesia a new religious fad that will blow over in time. Then there will be those who see some devious plot to overthrow traditional churches. And of course, many will find the contents to be true, but struggle with finding ways to live this out.

At Caesarea Philippi, Jesus asked His disciples, "Who do you say I am?" Peter's response was prompted by God Himself. A similar question is being posed to you, 'What is your response to what you have read?' What has the Holy Spirit spoken to you throughout this book?

Once you hear or read something, you become accountable for your response to it. You have every right to reject what I have written, but you do a grave disservice to yourself if you reject this without proving or disproving the facts. Even if you accept my assertions, it is still your responsibility to investigate the details (Acts 17:11).

> What is your response to what you have read?' What has the Holy Spirit spoken to you throughout this book?

Jesus said that He would build an ekklesia — not a church. Every word of God is true (Psalms 119:160; John 17:17). Jesus said He only repeated what the Father said (John 12:49; 14:10). God is not a man, that He should lie (Numbers 23:19; Hebrews 6:18). Therefore, three serious questions must be addressed.

1. Based on the original language of the New Testament, Jesus said He would build an ekklesia. Do we continue to accept the word 'church', knowing it is not what He said or intended?

2. Do we have a right to pursue anything other than what Jesus said?

3.  If we know that 'church' is a mistranslation of the word ekkle-
    sia, can we ignore this fact and continue doing 'church as
    usual'?

I will not attempt to answer these questions for you. You must
settle this in your own spirit. I believe we are on the very early stages
of a transition that will impact 'church' as we know it. I believe what
we know as 'church' will be dramatically different within the next ten
years. Some of the changes will be in response to social, political, and
economic pressure. But I believe the real change will take place when
believers embrace their true identity as the Lord's ekklesia, His powerful ruling council in the earth.

What happens next? You decide, my friend, because, LEAVING
CHURCH, in order to BECOME the Lord's EKKLESIA is in your hands.

Blessings!

# SUGGESTED RESOURCES

"The two most engaging powers of an author are
to make new things familiar, familiar things new"

William Makepeace Thackeray
19th Century English Novelist

EKKLESIA RISING: *The Authority of Christ in Communities of Contending Prayer* © 2014 by Dean Briggs Published by Champion Press Page 108

EKKLESIA: *The Government of the Kingdom of Heaven on Earth* ©2014 Joe Nicola Published by Spring Mill Publishing

BEYOND CHURCH: *An invitation to experience the lost word of the bible* © 2015 Steve Simms Published by Harper Simms Press

THE EKKLESIA: *The church that Jesus is building* © 2012 Anthony Daley Published by Creation House

EKKLESIA: *Rediscovering God's Instrument for Global Transformation* © 2014, 2017 Ed Silvoso Published by Chosen Books A Division of Baker Publishing Group

## OTHER BOOKS

UNFINISHED BUSINESS: *Returning The Ministry To The People Of God* © 1990, 2003 by Dr. Greg Ogden Published by Zondervan, Pages 130 – 155

THE SPONTANEOUS EXPANSION OF THE CHURCH: *and the Causes Which Hinder It* by Roland Allen. First Published 1927 Public Domain

CHURCH REFUGEES: *Sociologists reveal why people are DONE with the church but not their faith* © 2015 Josh Packard and Ashleigh Hope Published by group.com

MISSIONARY METHODS: *St Paul's or Ours?* By Roland Allen © 1962, World Dominion Press

# SUGGESTED RESOURCES

DEVELOPING APOSTOLIC STRATEGY: *8 Keys to Projecting Power in Every Sphere of Society* © 2010 Tim Taylor Published by Watchman Ministries International

PAGAN CHRISTIANITY? *Exploring the Roots of Our Church Practices* © 2002, 2008 by Frank Viola and George Barna Published by Tyndale. First printing by Present Testimony Ministry in 2002

NO LONGER CHURCH AS USUAL: *Restoring First Century Values and Structure to the 21ˢᵗ Century Church* Second Edition © 2013 T. Lemoss Kurtz Published by Kingdom Word Publications

## ONLINE REFERENCES ARE ACTIVE AS OF THE DATE OF PUBLICATION

http://www.greatsite.com/timeline-english-bible-history/king-james.html

https://gotquestions.org/Bishops-Bible.html

https://www.britannica.com/topic/divine-right-of-kings

http://www.wwnorton.com/college/history/ralph/workbook/ralprs20.htm

https://www.bl.uk/collection-items/the-true-law-of-free-monarchies-by-king-james-vi-and-i

https://www.ecclesia.org/truth/ekklesia.html

http://www.kjvonly.org/other/kj_instructs.htm

http://sidroth.org/articles/church-isnt-new-testament/

## OTHER RESOURCES

Atkerson, Steve [Editor], *House Church: simple – strategic – scriptural* © 2008 New Testament Reformation Fellowship

Barna, George *Revolution: Finding Vibrant Faith Beyond the Wall of the Sanctuary*, Tyndale House Publishers, Inc.

# SUGGESTED RESOURCES

Beckham, *William A. The Second Reformation: Reshaping the Church for the 21ˢᵗ Century*, Touch Publications

Bismark, Tudor *Order in the House: Establishing God's Governmental Structure in the Church and Beyond*, Truebrand Marketing Group

Bismark, Tudor *Reformation in the House: An Apostolic Model for the 21ˢᵗ Century Church*, Truebrand Marketing Group

Briggs, Dean *Ekklesia Rising: The Authority of Christ in Communities of Contending Prayer*, Champion Press

Bright, John *The Kingdom of God*, Abingdon Press

Bruce, F.F. *Paul: Apostle of the Heart Set Free*, William B. Eerdmans Publishing Company

Castellanos, Cesar *Successful Leadership through the Government of 12: Revised Edition*, G12 Publishers

Choudrie, Victor *Greet the Ekklesia: The Church in Your House*, English Addition July 2006

Clements, Dr. Kirby *A Philosophy of Ministry*, Publisher unknown

Clements, Dr. Kirby *When Prophecies Fail: A Practical Response to the Voice of God*, Clement Family Ministries

Cole, Neil *Organic Church: growing faith where life happens*, Jossey Bass

Cooke, Graham/Goodell, Gary *Permission Granted: to do Church differently in the 21ˢᵗ Century*, Destiny Image ® Publishers

Dale, Felicity *Getting Started, second edition* Karis Publishing

Daley, Anthony D. *The Ekklesia*, Creation House

David, Jonathan *Apostolic Strategies Affecting Nations*, 1997 Edition

Eckhardt, John *Moving in the Apostolic*, Renew Books Gospel Light

Eckhardt, John *Presbyteries and Apostolic Teams*, Crusaders Ministries

Eckhardt, John *The Ministry Anointing of the Apostle*, Crusaders Ministries

# SUGGESTED RESOURCES

Fenn, John *Return of the first Church: the open door to His Glory* © 2007 John Fenn Dog Ear Publishing

Getz, Gene A. *Elders and Leaders: God's Plan for Leading the Church: A Biblical, Historical and Cultural Perspective*, Moody Publishers

Hamon, Dr. Bill *Apostles Prophets and the Coming Moves of God: God's End-Time Plans for His Church and Planet Earth*, Destiny Image ® Publishers

Hamon, Dr. Bill *The Day of the Saints: Equipping Believers for their Revolutionary Role in Ministry*, Destiny Image ® Publishers

Hamon, Dr. Bill *The Eternal Church: A Prophetic Look at the Church – Her History, Restoration, and Destiny*, Destiny Image ® Publisher

Hamon, Dr. Bill, *Prophets Pitfalls and Principles: God's Prophetic People Today*, Destiny Image ® Publishers

Hamon, Jane *The Cyrus Decree: Releasing apostolic and prophetic keys to the twenty-first century Church to liberate captives, transfer wealth, revolutionize nations and build the Kingdom of God*, Christian International Family Church

Joyner, Rick *A Prophetic Vision for the 21st Century: A Spiritual Map to Help You Navigate into the Future*, Thomas Nelson Publishers

Kraybill, Donald B. *The Upside Down Kingdom*, Herald Press

Krieder, Larry/Myer, Ron/Prokopchak, Steve/Sauder, Brian *The Biblical Role of Elders for Today's Church: New Testament leadership principles for equipping elders*, House to House Publications

Kurtz, Tim *How to discover your Calling, Purpose & Ministry*, Kingdom Word Publications

Munroe, Myles *God's Big Idea: Reclaiming God's Original Purpose for Your Life*, Destiny Image ® Publishers

Nee, Watchman *The NORMAL CHRISTIAN CHURCH LIFE: The New Testament Pattern of the Churches, the Ministry, and the Work*, Living Stream Ministry

# SUGGESTED RESOURCES

Richards, E. Randolph and Brandon J. O'Brien, *Misreading Scripture With Western Eyes: Removing Cultural Blinders to Better Understand the Bible*, Intervarsity Press

Rutz, James *Mega Shift*, Empowerment Press

Rutz, James *Open Church*, Empowerment Press

Sapp, Roger *The Last Apostles on Earth*, All Nations Publications

Simson, Wolfgang *Houses That Change the World: The return of the house churches*, Authentic Books

Slaughter, Michael *Spiritual Entrepreneurs: 6 Principles for Risking Renewal*, Abingdon Press

Slaughter, Michael/Bird, Warren *unLearing Church: just when you thought you had leadership all figured out*, Group Publishing

Trueblood, Elton *The Company of the Committed: A bold and imaginative rethinking of the strategy of the Church in contemporary life*, Harper & Row Publishers

Viola, Frank *So You Want To Start A House Church? First Century Style Church Planting For Today*, Present Testimony Ministry

Weston, Charles Gilbert *The Seven Covenants: A Study of The Bible Through The Seven Great Covenants of The Scriptures*, Weston Bible Ministries

Wohlberg, Steve *End Time Delusions: The Rapture, the Antichrist, Israel, and the End of the World*, Treasure House/Destiny Image ® Publishers

# Appendix A

## 12 Principles For Home Gatherings

**The goal: become an active ruling council that demonstrates the values and structure of first century Christianity.**

Making a transition can be a daunting endeavor. You are learning how become an ekklesia or ruling council. There will be times when you will feel completely unsure of your activities. You may have friends and relatives who question what you are doing, and you feel inadequate to answer their questions.

It's okay to feel this way early on. As you learn more, you will become more confident. The most important thing now is that you know that you are in the will of God. You must know that what you are doing (gathering with believers in a home) can be confirmed by the Word of God.

Over the last two years, we have been transitioning into a network of interdependent house gatherings. Each of the gatherings that have been birthed out of our ministry is unique. My wife and I host gatherings in our home primarily to build and encourage those who have gatherings in their homes. These wonderful saints have exhibited growth and maturing, and those who attend their gatherings always leave uplifted

The following 12 principles are based on activities and lessons learned by the various groups among us. These principles are drawn from real experiences, and will help you navigate this process.

1. **IT'S OKAY TO MEET ON DAYS OTHER THAN SUNDAY, AND AT TIMES OTHER THAN II A.M.**

   Like most believers, we have been programmed to 'go to church' every Sunday morning. Now that you are primarily meeting in homes, you may feel a little out of place at first, but rest assured, there is no scripture that mandates that you meet on Sundays. Meet at a time that is most convenient for you and the sisters and brothers in your gathering (Colossians 2:16).

2. **IT IS NOT THE PLACE – IT IS THE PURPOSE**

   The primary place believers met was in the home. You are no less spiritual because you gather in a home rather than a dedicated building. Remember you are allowing the Holy Spirit to build a 'family' not an organization (John 4:21-23).

   Your primary purpose early on is to understand as much as you can about the ekklesia and to get to know each other. This would be apostolic doctrine and fellowship (Acts 2:42). Share and grow together.

3. **YOU ARE GATHERING TO 'LIVE LIFE' AMONG OTHER BELIEVERS**

   Those who gather with you are your family. You are not 'members' of an organization – you are a living organic body of believers. We recommend that you gather at least two or three times every month. However, your relationships should extend beyond the times you get together (ICorinthians 12:25-26). Make a strong and intentional effort be involved in the lives of your sisters and brothers throughout the week. Attend social events together, visit each school functions, provide assistance such as rides to work, babysitting or babysitting when possible. The list can go on. The key point is don't simply settle for seeing and ministering to each other when you meet as a group.

188

4.  COMMIT TO BUILDING TRUST AMONG EACH OTHER

    The more you gather, the more you will learn about each other.

    1.  You build trust with each other as you keep each other's personal matters confidential, and pray for each other's needs.

    2.  You build trust by being open and honest with one another in love (Romans 12:13-15; James 5:16).

    3.  You build trust by committing to work through misunderstandings and disagreements, if they occur. Don't let division be among you. Be diligent to prayerfully seek solutions together. Don't allow satan any room for dissention.

    4.  Don't allow doctrinal differences to bring division. Find ways to equitably search out the Word of God rather than allow doctrine to divide you. Appendix B are the primary values that the ekklesia should embrace.

    5.  You build trust by refusing to allow anyone outside of your gathering to disparage or criticize anyone in your fellowship.

5.  IN EVERY GATHERING, BE INTENTIONAL ABOUT EDIFYING, EXHORTING AND COMFORTING ONE ANOTHER.

    Prophecy edifies the church (1 Corinthians 14:3). Every time you gather with your brothers and sisters, seek ways to build life in each other. Always seek ways to encourage each other. Consider every person as someone valuable to the Kingdom of God.

6.  EVERY GATHERING MAY NOT BE THE SAME – FOLLOW THE HOLY SPIRIT LEADING

    Don't get locked into a format. The Holy Spirit leads your gathering. One week you may find yourself discussing scripture. Another week may be all praise, prayer and worship. Then there may be times when all you do is fellowship with each other.

7. **DON'T LOOK FOR ONE PERSON TO 'PREACH' OR TEACH DURING YOUR REGULAR GATHERINGS**

   Whenever you gather, everybody should have something to contribute. The strength of New Testament gatherings is everyone allowing Christ in them to connect with Christ in others. Allow the gifts of the Spirit to flow through you (1 Corinthians 12:7; 14:26). Attend each gathering ready to share what God has shown you.

8. **DON'T PUT TIME LIMITS ON YOUR GATHERING**

   Your gathering is a family of believers. You are living life among each other. Being cognizant of your time is not the same as setting time limits on your gathering. Spend whatever time you need. Some gatherings may be shorter or longer than others. The key thing is to allow the Holy Spirit to work His work among you.

9. **SHARE A FELLOWSHIP MEAL**

   Whether it be a potluck, a barbeque, or just a few finger snacks, eat together each time you gather. There is no set time to eat. Some groups eat before they have any ministry time, others eat before they leave, and still others just set the food out and people eat throughout the time together. Do what is most comfortable for you; just make sure you eat.

10. **SHARE THE LORD'S TABLE AT EVERY GATHERING**

    Depending on your 'church' background, this can be controversial and uncomfortable for some. This is because many have been taught that

'Communion', the Eucharist, or the Lord's Table can only be adminis-tered by an 'ordained clergy'. To limit this to 'clergy' cannot be sub-stantiated by scripture. This is an ordinance for all believers.

For more information, you may consider getting a copy of THE LORD'S TABLE, one of the first booklets we released in our Apos-tolic Doctrine series. This booklet will give you the basic understanding you need, as well as suggestions as to how you can do this in your gath-erings. It is a sacred act, but yet simple. Religion has made is so mystical that some people actually fear it.

The Lord's Table is one of the greatest and blessed things you can do at your gatherings.

## 11. UTILIZE THE RESOURCES AVAILABLE

Clearly this is new to many. Therefore, we have provided a list of re-sources that my help you more. Take advantage of them. Prayerfully, we are seeking innovative ways to help minister to people around the country. We will be doing teleconferences, webinars and utilize any tools we can to strengthen you.

As we train various ministry gifts, we encourage you to utilize them to help you be effective in your calling, purpose and ministry.

## 12. PRAY

Pray at all times. This book, or any other book you read, cannot take the place of the Word of God, or the work of the Holy Spirit in you. Seek the Lord every step of the way. In your gatherings, pray with each other and for each other. Pray that the Lord will reveal His ekklesia in your area, and ultimately in the earth. Pray for lost souls. And I humbly ask that you pray for our ministry work, that we will accomplish all the Lord has called us to do.

# APPENDIX B

## THE NEW TESTAMENT VALUES

Sound doctrine is important for all believers. However, it must be understood that doctrine in the first century strengthened the believers, whereas doctrine today divides believers. Jesus prayed that we would be one (John 17:21). Paul admonished the Corinthian believers to be perfectly joined together in the same mind and judgment. Throughout the book of Acts we read accounts of believers being of one mind, one soul, and being on one accord (Acts 2:1, 46; 4:32; 5:12).

Scripture admonishes us to speak things that belong to sound doctrine (Titus 2:1). The ekklesia were taught the Doctrine of Christ (Hebrews 6:1-2), and avidly followed the Apostles Doctrine (Acts 2:42). Even with all their flaws and missteps, these believers impacted the earth with such power that it was reported that they turned the world upside down (Acts 17:6).

As this transition from church to ekklesia becomes more pronounced in the earth, it is critical that believers embrace the values found in the first century. Doctrine brought clarity to these values. These five core values are summarized here, and you are encouraged to memorize them and to spend time learning how to express them in your daily walk with Christ Jesus.

## I. THE LORDSHIP OF JESUS CHRIST

Jesus is Lord! Every knee shall bow, every tongue must confess the Lordship of Jesus Christ (Philippians 2:11).Salvation is impossible without first acknowledging that Jesus is Lord (Romans 9:9). The Holy Spirit empowers you to say, "Jesus is Lord" (I Corinthians 12:3). If we miss, misunderstand or neglect this first and primary value, then everything else we do is null and void. There is no reason to discuss any other value if we overlook this first and primary value – the Lordship of Jesus Christ.

## 2. THE PRIESTHOOD OF EVERY BELIEVER

The priesthood of the believer must be understood in functional terms rather than in titles. God sees us as kings and priests. It is not important that we are called priests, it is only important that we do what the priests are called to do. To be a priest unto the Lord is to minister TO Him and not FOR Him. It is when we acknowledge Christ in each other. It is allowing each person to express Christ as He is revealed within them. More importantly, it is submitting to that expression of Christ in our brothers and sisters.

## 3. THE HOLY SPIRIT – HIS ACTS AND HIS GIFTS

Jesus is Lord over His ekklesia. The Holy Spirit is the sole managing agent of His ekklesia in the earth. No decision should be made, or action taken if it is not directed by the Holy Spirit. Being filled with the Holy Spirit was normative for first century believers. It is also normal for believers today. His grace, spiritual and ministry gifts are the divine tools He entrusts to believers to accomplish the work of ministry in the earth today.

## 4. GROWING SPIRITUALLY AND NUMERICALLY THROUGH COVENANT RELATIONSHIPS

Growth, spiritual and numerical, is a value we must embrace. A healthy body grows. Individuals must grow in grace, and in the knowledge of Jesus Christ (2Peter 3:18). Equally, believers must grow in covenant relationship with each other.

In the Kingdom Mandate (Genesis 1:28), we are commanded to multiply and fill the earth. It is through covenant relationships that this command becomes possible. Jesus said the greatest command is that "[we] should love the Lord our God with all our heart, and with all our soul, and with all our mind, and with all our strength: this is the first commandment. And the second is like, namely this, [we must] love [our] neighbor as [ourselves]. There is none other commandment greater than these (Mark 12:30-31). Jesus further said that the world would know we are His disciples as we exhibit our love for each other (John 13:35).

5. NO ONE AMONG US SHALL LACK

The principle behind '*no one lacking*' is that I will lay down my possessions for the benefit of other believers. Our goal is more than meeting their needs in the time of crisis. It is to insure that they do not lack so that they can function in the body more effectively. *No one lacking* is not an empty promise to pay bills, provide food or make believers wealthy, but rather a practice geared to make every believer productive.

Made in the USA
Coppell, TX
31 August 2020

35934083R00115